A John Catt Publication

The third edition of the bestsellin

Leadership Matters 3.0

How leaders at all levels can create great schools

Andy Buck

Now organised into 40 practical topics

"Much more than a how-to guide. Impressive synthesis of evidence-based theory and down-to-earth advice"
Dame Alison Peacock

LEADERSHIP MATTERS
With You, For You

First published 2018

by John Catt Educational Ltd,
15 Riduna Park, Station Road,
Melton, Woodbridge IP12 1QT

Tel: +44 (0) 1394 389850 Fax: +44 (0) 1394 386893
Email: enquiries@johncatt.com
Website: www.johncatt.com

ISBN: 978 1 911 382 88 1

Set and designed by John Catt Educational Limited

Praise for *Leadership Matters*

'Andy's latest book is a masterpiece, combining the vast expertise and experience he gained as a teacher and school leader with his extensive knowledge of the most useful theory and research into leadership.' Brian Lightman, former general secretary of ASCL

'A very powerful tool in the hands of school leaders who are determined to do the best for young people.' Chris Husbands, Vice Chancellor, Sheffield Hallam University and former Director of UCL Institute of Education

'This book is an important contribution to the mission we all need to commit to: developing school leaders of the present and the future.' Emma Knights, Chief Executive, National Governors Association

'I cannot think of a more useful book on school leadership. It is full of good sense and practical suggestions, with a strong theoretical underpinning.' John Dunford, former general secretary of the Association of School and College Leaders

'Alive with real examples, this book is – unusually – both an easy-to-apply practical guide and a stimulus for new thinking and fresh possibilities.' Jon Coles, Chief Executive, United Learning

'Rarely will you see the complexities of leadership and management made this clear and translated into a book this useful. Each school leader and would-be leader should pick up a copy.' Alex Quigley, Director of Learning and Research, Huntington School, author of *The Confident Teacher*

'A must read for school leaders. Comprehensive and packed full of evidence and practical wisdom on the characteristics of successful leaders.' James Toop, CEO, Ambition School Leadership

'Typically accessible, with practical advice and some excellent analysis and personal insights it is a useful resource for reading in chunks as and when or in one sitting as you prepare for a new challenge. It made me wince and nod within the same chapters as I recognised my traits, successes and mistakes.' Professor Toby Salt, CEO, AQA

'This is an invaluable resource for school leaders not only in the UK but from further afield – highly recommended.' Susan Douglas, Senior Adviser, Schools, British Council and CEO, Eden Academy

'Andy Buck has created an easy-to-read yet immensely powerful guide for every school leader, a book filled with wisdom, humour and practical guidance. He manages to reach a perfect balance: a mix of inspiration with occasional uncomfortable truths to confront. This is a must-read.' David Weston, Chief Executive, The Teacher Development Trust

'A clear and compelling argument that collaboration within our schools and across schools fosters strategic thinking and healthy reflection.' Jill Berry, Leadership Consultant, author

'Andy Buck has been there and done it and this book is evidence of that, bringing together a range of leadership thinking and practical in-school experience that delivers a practical,useful handbook for school leaders everywhere.' John Campbell, Executive Director, Growth Coaching International, Sydney, Australia

For Jo and Wendy

My loving, funny and adorable twin sisters.

Thank you for being my pupils when
I taught my very first lesson!

Contents

Foreword

I am delighted to recommend this book to you. Leadership is complex, demanding and of vital importance. Within this book Andy Buck offers boundless practical strategies, resources and tools for reflection, always written with a tone of humility and gentle humour. He reflects on the journey towards achieving great leadership, drawing on his own experience of the 'Good to Great' programme of the London Challenge, headship and the evidence that exists within the literature about ways of building and sustaining a positive high performing culture and climate of shared values. We are provided with a rich seam of solutions to the ever challenging aspects of leadership in a manner that is fuelled by the importance of evidence-informed strategy.

As the Chief Executive of the Chartered College of Teaching, I am all too aware of the necessity of building leadership opportunities across the education system that enable our teachers to thrive. Leaders who can build organisations driven by shared ambition imbued with positivity and emotional intelligence are likely to be those that create the best possible environment for both colleagues and young people to achieve success. There are currently many pressures upon school leaders, one of which may be to reach for the solution that appears to offer a quick-fix. Within this book we are reminded of the vital importance of building and sustaining a culture that enables us to recognise the importance of key development areas such as alignment of vision that enable others to flourish. These approaches take time, but the advice and strategies offered ensure that every step taken will contribute to the ultimate aim of building a resilient, principled team capable of achieving their goals.

We are offered sensible down-to-earth practical advice throughout. It is particularly helpful to read the distilled findings of establish academics and to hear from many thought-leaders in the field of leadership both within and beyond the field of education. Each chapter begins with an inspirational quote followed by detailed examples that support what Andy Buck describes as 'leadership habits'. Many chapters contain a useful synthesis of theory about particular aspects of leadership such as change management, dealing with conflict, building alignment and self-knowledge. The importance of developing trust through organisational listening and coaching skills is emphasised throughout.

This is not a 'how-to' guide. It is much more than that. Within these pages the reader is at times both inspired and challenged. No-where in this book is there an expectation that leadership should be simply instinctive or that it can easily learned. Recognition is given throughout of the complexity of skills needed to lead with heart and head. Wherever you are in your leadership journey, this book will help you reflect, take stock, and move forward with professional courage. Keep reading, we need you, our children need you and our teachers need the kind of leadership that Andy Buck shows us it is possible to achieve.

Dame Alison Peacock,
CEO, Chartered College of Teaching

Introduction

Never doubt that a small group of thoughtful,
concerned citizens can change the world.
Indeed, it is the only thing that ever has.
Margaret Mead

When I started teaching geography in a north London comprehensive school back in 1987, I was passionate about my subject. I had been in training for a year at the Institute of Education in London and had learned a huge amount from my inspirational tutors, Frances Slater and David Lambert. I loved the pupils in my school and I loved my job. But even then, I knew how my own success depended upon others around me. There were times when I needed to draw on more experienced colleagues in the school when dealing with difficult pupils. If our pupils were to have a coherent and challenging educational experience that enabled them to achieve great things, there needed to be proper planning and organisation of the curriculum as a whole. If I was to continue to grow and develop as a teacher, I needed the chance to work with others in a productive and focused way that enabled me to reflect on my practice and improve. In other words, even then, I knew that I needed to be working as part of a well-orchestrated team: that leadership mattered.

These days, of course, it is pretty widely accepted that second to the quality of teaching itself, the single thing that makes the biggest difference to outcomes for pupils is leadership. So this book isn't about *why* leadership in schools matters. It is about what great leadership *looks like* at all levels, both within schools and beyond them. It unashamedly aims to cover leadership in a huge range of contexts. As a school leader reading this, you may be at the beginning of your own leadership journey, taking your very first steps into middle leadership. You may be a senior leader or the head of a school. You may even be a system leader with a role working across more than one school, leading a trust, federation or an alliance of schools.

From my experience, while the focus of your work as leader will undoubtedly shift according to your role, many of the key elements of great leadership are present at every level, regardless of your experience or sphere of influence. All that differs is your context. To say otherwise, in my view, is to over-complicate the issue. Great leadership is the same, however senior you happen to be. What matters most is how you apply that understanding of your situation to be able to focus your leadership actions and approach to suit your context. For example, a brand-new head of English or leader of literacy across a school needs to quickly assess the capacity of the teachers delivering this important curriculum area before deciding what the team needs to do next as well as how, as a leader, they should approach making this change happen. If capacity and expertise is low, the right approach may very well be quite directive. On the other hand, if the team is more experienced and highly competent, such an approach is likely to backfire. This is no different from a headteacher taking over a new school, working out what the strategic priorities need to be over the next three to five years and how best to implement them. The only difference is the scale.

So the approach of this book is to take an evidence-based look at what great school leadership looks like and allow you to translate this into the context you are working in. My own experience has shown me the power of this approach, particularly in recent years, where my work has given me a privileged insight into hundreds of schools. Where a school or group of schools see the potential of leaders collaborating, with a shared set of values, goals and ways of working, there is no limit to the outcomes for pupils, so long as leaders can take their agreed shared approaches and modify them to suit their situation.

In thinking about what makes a great school, I have drawn heavily on my learning from the time I was leading the London Challenge *Good to Great* (G2G) programme. This book aims to synthesise that learning with my knowledge and experience of school leadership more generally, drawing on examples from the schools I have worked in and had the pleasure to work alongside over the last 30 years. It aims to break down this learning into discrete, easily digestible chunks or topics. For each topic, I will map out the opportunities and challenges you may well be facing right now in your current role, providing you with useful theory and background to help you bring out the best in yourself and those around you.

To allow you to apply this learning in your context, I will use the terms team, colleagues or staff quite a lot. These can mean different things, depending on your situation, so feel free to apply these as appropriate depending on your own role:

Middle leaders: when I use these terms, I am usually referring to those staff that are in the team you lead or upon whom you rely for delivery if you have a whole-school responsibility.

Senior leaders: when I am talking about your team, colleagues or staff, I am usually referring to those you line-manage or upon whom you rely to deliver your whole-school responsibility. This may include all staff at times.

Heads (and for heads, read principals or heads of school): I am usually referring to the members of your senior team. It may sometimes also refer to middle leaders and the wider staff team.

System leaders: someone who is running a group of schools. In this context your colleagues are likely to be the heads of each school and sometimes the senior teams in each. Occasionally it will refer to all the staff in all your schools.

Governors and/or trustees: depending on your context, these terms may relate to the single governing board of your school, the board of trustees of your multi-academy trust or federation or the 'local' governance for one school within a multi-academy or federated group of schools. In whichever context, these references are about the important oversight and vital contribution such governance provides.

Similarly, when I talk about **schools**, I am using the word generically to include all schools, academies, free schools, special schools and colleges who are educating pupils from early years to aged 19.

It is also worth mentioning that, while I have just separated out the five different levels of leadership, I wish to make it quite explicit that the book is written with all five in mind. In my view, the more that a school thinks of its leadership capacity existing within a single leadership team, the better. It may sound like I am contradicting myself, but my point is this: all leaders in any school need to feel they are part of a single leadership effort, with a shared set of values and ways of working. Otherwise, you end up with frequent misunderstanding and unproductive tensions. You also lose the opportunity for more senior leaders to coach and mentor their less experienced colleagues with the same goals and ambitions in mind. It's why, when I work with schools on leadership development and team building, I won't work with groups of middle leaders unless all the senior leaders in the school are involved too. Experience has taught us that if senior leaders aren't part of this shared experience, the process has significantly reduced impact, not just because senior leaders don't have access to the language and concepts discussed, but because there is a 'them and us' culture that just seems to get in the way.

Topic 1

Leadership Matters overview

Leadership is a choice, not a position.
Stephen Covey

Section A: Personal qualities

Section A of this book provides an opportunity for you to reflect on your personal qualities. What is the moral purpose and motivation that sits behind your approach? Who are you as a leader? How do you tend to respond in certain situations? How well do you know yourself and how able are you to manage your emotions? How do you respond when the going gets tough? These personal characteristics will have a strong influence over your effectiveness every single day. School leaders are not immune from basic things going wrong. When you have a tough day and, if you teach, one of your own lessons has been a bit of a disaster or you have had a really challenging and unsuccessful meeting with a difficult member of staff, how you manage your own emotions and remain positive is important. Your staff need you to remain optimistic in such situations, even when there appears to be absolutely no reason to do so!

For all leaders, having a strong sense of one's own personal characteristics is a hugely powerful and affirming base from which to lead, particularly when the challenges of a school leadership role have the potential to become all-consuming.

Section B: Your situation

Section B of the book is all about the importance of context. This is probably the moment to consider what I have named the 'giraffe concept'. From an early age you have probably learned that the reason giraffes have evolved to have long necks is so they can reach the leaves on trees that other animals can't. The long neck is the key thing that enables them to be successful and it's the same for them all. But a quick look at giraffes across the world reveals that, while they may all share similarly long necks, their markings can vary considerably. Some are dark, some lighter. Some have large patches of colour, some smaller. The markings vary according to their environment and the age of the giraffe. They have evolved to suit their context. For me, the same principle applies to school leadership. As a leader, you need to be clear what the leadership *long neck* issues are: the things about leadership you need to know and understand to ensure success. But you also need to understand your context, your own predispositions and be able to adapt to them to suit your situation, both in terms of what you need to do and how you do it.

Figure 1: The giraffe concept

Of course, the giraffe concept doesn't just apply to leadership. It is equally relevant when it comes to other facets of education, for example teaching strategies. As Dylan Wiliam (2015) argues, 'In education, "*what works?*" is not really the right question because everything works somewhere and nothing works everywhere. So what's interesting, what's important in education is: "*under what conditions does this work?*"' School leaders, with their staff, need to use the very best evidence to make sure they are using approaches that suit their context.

Section C: Leadership actions

Whether you are running a group of schools or have just taken on your first middle leadership role, the job is basically the same. Steve Radcliffe, in his brilliantly intuitive *Leadership: plain and simple* (2012), argues that leadership is really only about doing three key things well, which he summarises as Future-Engage-Deliver or 'FED'. As a former school leader myself, the simplicity of his framework is immediately appealing. The more we keep things simple, the better!

In the FED model, the first key area focuses on the future you envisage for your organisation as a whole or your individual team. It relates to your shared vision: what you want your team or organisation to achieve together. Of course, this needs to be backed up with a clear approach to managing those changes in a way that makes the best use of your resources, both financial and human. Ideally, the overall strategy will be based on what research and evidence tell you are most effective, and the degree to which you are keen to try out and evaluate new ideas for yourself. For those of you in system leadership roles, this is about the strategy underpinning how a group of schools can work together successfully. For a middle leader, it's about translating wider organisational goals into something tangible and ambitious for your front-line team.

Importantly, Radcliffe argues that for you to be most successful as a leader, you really need to care about your vision or goal. In other words, to use his delightful turn of phrase, you need to be 'up to something'. Getting a powerful match between what you are good at and passionate about, and the goals of your team or organisation can make a huge difference to how successful you will be. Without this, he argues, there's no guarantee of achieving meaningful progress.

Once you are clear on your vision for the future and your strategy for getting there, the next key area of work is to build and sustain great relationships. Only if you engage effectively with others can you as leaders at any level make change happen. For heads, having a team of staff who are committed to your shared goals and work effectively together to support one another in achieving them, is at the heart of what makes a great school. In other words, this is all about getting a collective buy-in to what you want to achieve, and inspiring and enabling others to lead with you. As Radcliffe puts it, whatever role you are leading in, you need to make sure 'the relationships are big enough to get the job done'. Never was that maxim truer than in a school.

The third stage in the model is focused on making sure you deliver. Leadership isn't just about strategy and inspiring others. It's about making sure things happen when you want them to and to the standard you expect. Great schools are the result of great delivery, day-in, day-out. We know that one of the biggest challenges facing schools all over the world is how to create consistent delivery for every pupil, regardless of the curriculum area, their teacher, or their age. The degree of variation of pupil outcomes within schools is still greater than the difference that exists between them.

In a school context, great delivery comes from clear systems, processes and support, based on the evidence of what works. This enables your staff to be great at their jobs, especially your teachers. It's also about monitoring outcomes and progress in a way that ensures consistent delivery and promotes pupil learning.

The beauty of Steve Radcliffe's model is its absolute simplicity. But there is another leadership framework, created by David Pendleton (2012) which is very similar to FED and does, in effect, consider how each of the three elements interact with one another. For me, with a school context in mind, breaking leadership into slightly smaller chunks in this way is useful and certainly resonates with the reality of the job at any level. Figure 2 shows how the model works.

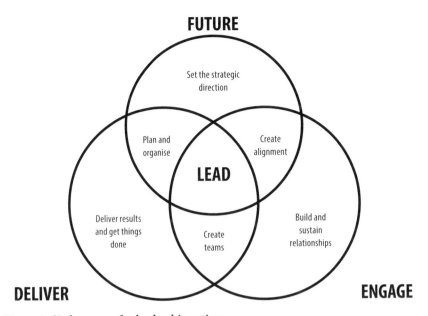

Figure 2: Six key areas for leadership action

Adapted from David Pendleton's Primary Colours model (2012) combined with Steve Radcliffe's Future-Engage-Deliver (2012)

As already mentioned, there are some important inter-plays between the three FED leadership areas. It's no good having a great strategy unless you have **planned and organised**. Planning ahead comes more easily to some leaders than others but is critical for us all. No school achieves excellence if the leaders that are responsible for bringing out the best in pupils and staff are poorly organised. Apart from the obvious confusion and inefficiency that results, the negative effect on individuals' motivation can also be very detrimental.

Secondly, you can lead the most harmonious and motivated team in the world, but if the individuals in it aren't clear on the shared direction in which you are headed, you won't achieve the ambitious goals you are striving for. Creating strong **alignment** is therefore critical and good communication is essential. Whatever level you are leading at, your staff will be much more effective if everyone is clear on where you are headed and has bought into the vision.

Finally, school leadership at any level is about leading a team of staff, not doing everything yourself. While it can be very tempting to take on tasks, partly because you know you can usually do the job quicker and better than others, great leaders **create teams**, delegating tasks and decisions to others. Empowering colleagues in this way, so long as it is done well, has the capacity to significantly increase the quality of delivery overall.

Leadership and management

Distinctions are often made about the difference between leadership and management. Both are critical for the success of a team, school or group of schools. As Peter Drucker (2007) helpfully suggests, 'Management is doing things right; leadership is doing the right things.' But in schools there are times when the distinction between the two can feel rather artificial. Where, for example, does a good coaching conversation sit? In my view, it is both. You are *leading* by asking great questions that are helping a colleague to develop and empowering them to lead too. You are *managing* by engaging in a conversation that is usually about improving delivery, performance and, ultimately, pupil impact.

Which is why David Pendleton's Primary Colours model and Steve Radcliffe's Future-Engage-Deliver model work so well. They both avoid making this distinction while at the same time covering the critical elements of each. If leadership is about doing the right things, then there are key elements that relate to strategy. But both also give proper attention to delivery and making things happen, and happen well. The link between the two is great engagement with those who will make this all happen. This book takes the same approach. The focus is on providing models and guidance that leaders at all levels can apply to their context, rather than providing technical descriptions of management techniques such as financial planning and budgeting.

Section D: Leadership approach

Ultimately, the actions that you take as a leader are critical. What you do to create strategy, build relationships and ensure strong delivery will underpin the success of your staff and therefore your pupils. But it is not quite as simple as that. Your success as a leader at any level isn't just about what you do. It's also about how you lead: your leadership style and how you support and inspire others to develop. Section D of the book discusses the importance for leaders at all levels to be able to adapt their leadership approach to suit their context. From my experience, this usually boils down to properly understanding the performance, the people and how much time you have! Central to success in this area is developing the critical leadership habit of *asking first*. Using a coaching leadership approach, at least to start with in a conversation, can unlock a much deeper understanding of any situation, enabling adjustments to then be made to both what you decide to do and how you decide to do it. Getting your leadership approach right has the potential to significantly enhance the impact of what you do for all those you work with.

Culture and climate

What you do as a school leader makes a difference to the results you achieve, however you choose to define what you mean by results. But the relationship between leadership and results isn't direct. As Figure 3 suggests, the actions you take as a leader have a significant impact on the culture and climate within your sphere of influence.

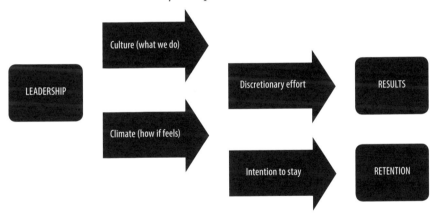

Figure 3: Leadership and results
Adapted from the Corporate Leadership Council (2004)

In this context, *culture* is taken to mean 'the way we do things around here' and relates to systems, procedures, and common practices as well as the high standards and expectations that exist in the way these are delivered. A useful way of thinking of culture is to consider what someone new joining your team would see happening on a day-to-day basis and the extent to which everyone in the team is working in the same way and to the same level of expectation. Is there a consistent set of high expectations from you about how your team should work? As a result of this, for example, are the learning environments you oversee inspiring and well organised? Do pupils have strong and supportive relationships with their peers and all the staff they work with?

Climate is more about how it feels to work in a team. For your team, this reflects its morale, how appreciated your team of staff feel and the degree of trust within the team as whole. This is much more difficult to describe or measure, but there is evidence to suggest that the effect of climate on team productivity is considerable. This is explored in more detail in the next topic.

Discretionary effort

Taken together, the more positive the culture and climate you create, the more likely your team of staff are to go the extra mile. This concept is known as *discretionary effort*. It is commonly described as the input from individuals over and above that which they need to contribute in order to keep their jobs. Critical in this context, however, is that the effort individuals make is directed productively. You will probably know of well-meaning and hard-working colleagues who regrettably did not have the impact that their efforts deserved because they were too often focused on doing the wrong things. In a classroom context, it's all very well having fantastically enjoyable lessons if what the pupils are learning doesn't relate to the curriculum they are meant to be following or the assessments they will have to take.

In other words, it's not about working longer or harder. That way lie the issues of stress, burn-out and disaffection that mean too many people leave the profession. It's about caring about one's work in a way that means individuals are constantly striving to improve, to be a tiny bit better tomorrow than they were yesterday.

Getting the culture and climate right can therefore also have an impact on an individual's intention to stay at a school, which in turn affects overall retention levels. If you accept the argument that a bigger problem for many school systems is retention not recruitment, then getting these basics conditions right is crucial for both schools and the wider system.

Pulling this all together

Figure 4 sums up the overall Leadership Matters framework. It forms the basis for the structure of the rest of the book.

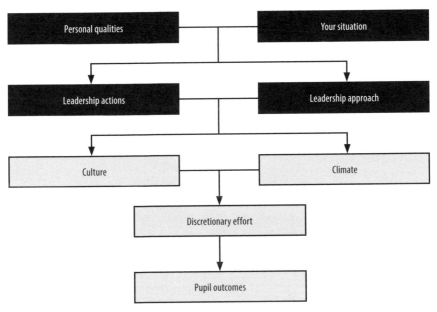

Figure 4: The Leadership Matters model

Leadership starts with you. Your understanding of yourself: the way you tend to behave in certain situations, what you enjoy and are good at and those areas you should probably focus on if you want to improve your effectiveness. But you also need to take the time to properly understand your situation: the people and the context you find yourself in.

Taken together, an understanding of self and situation should enable you to decide what actions you need to prioritise and the best approach to take in implementing them. If you get this right, you will create a productive culture and climate that combine to release significant discretionary effort from those you lead which will lead to you achieving the pupil outcomes you aspire to.

You will notice that the first four tiles are shaded. This reflects the fact that they are the key areas where school leaders can make changes that will make a difference. The remaining topics in the book are grouped under these four areas, with each representing the four key sections of the book. Section C, which focuses on leadership actions is considerably larger than the other sections, reflecting the fact that most important facet of leadership is what you actually do!

Taken together, the outcome of the changes you make in all these areas will lead to the positive differences in culture, climate and discretionary effort that will bring you the results you seek to achieve.

Key points

- Do you take time to properly understand your situation before acting?
- How do you make sure you properly understand your own predispositions?
- What is your balance like across the different areas of leadership actions?
- What do you do to build discretionary effort?

Topic 2

Discretionary effort

What everyone in the astronaut corps
shares in common is not gender or
ethnic background, but motivation,
perseverance, and desire – the desire to
participate in a voyage of discovery.
Ellen Ochoa

The previous topic outlined what we mean by discretionary effort and
where it fits within the wider Leadership Matters model. As the diagram
below reminds us, discretionary effort is the product of the culture and
climate that our leadership creates.

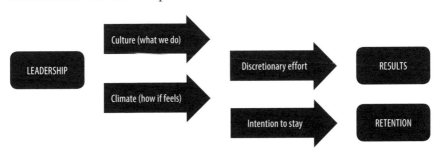

Figure 5: Leadership and results
Adapted from the Corporate Leadership Council (2004)

While the rest of the book sets out in more detail the leadership actions and approaches needed to create a strong culture and climate, this topic focuses on the key things that appear to be the most effective at building discretionary effort.

The Corporate Leadership Council (2004) carried out a survey of organisations of all types from across the world, looking into what builds engagement in employees. As part of this work, it asked thousands of participants how much effect each of nine key actions that organisations undertake to build discretionary effort had on their levels of motivation. The table below shows what people said. Each percentage represents an average of the maximum total impact of all the strategies within a category. The maximum total impact for any given strategy is calculated by comparing two statistical estimates: the predicted discretionary effort level for an employee who scores 'high' on the strategy, and the predicted discretionary effort level for an employee who scores 'low' on the strategy. The impact of each strategy is modelled separately.

1. Bonus pay	2%
2. In work benefits	10%
3. Personal development	12%
4. I am a good fit for my job	17%
5. Senior team characteristics	17%
6. Induction	20%
7. Organisational culture	21%
8. Line manager characteristics	25%

Figure 6: Factors that affect engagement
Corporate Leadership Council (2004)

It's interesting to note how bonus pay is such a low motivator, especially given that this survey was carried out in businesses as well as in other settings such as schools, hospitals and charities. It is also interesting to see how important induction appears to be. I imagine this is because an individual's first impression of an organisation sticks and can have a profound effect on their assessment of the quality of the culture and expectations. My final reflection is on the importance of the line manager. This is particularly significant for larger schools, where this is basically suggesting that it is middle leaders – who line manage most of the staff in – that have the ability to influence discretionary effort more than anyone else. It's no wonder middle leadership is often referred to as the engine-room of larger schools. In smaller schools, I imagine the senior leadership team and line manager categories are probably one and the same!

As with all evidence like this, it is important to recognise its limitations around context, but it certainly offers some useful food for thought.

So what is it that school leaders can do that can make the biggest difference to discretionary effort? Each of the tiles in the diagram below contains ideas that I believe build engagement. Some, like clarity, are not that exciting, but are absolutely crucial when it comes to creating buy-in. If people don't know what is expected of them, the required culture will not develop and discretionary effort will inevitably be reduced. Others, like openness, transparency and trust are more about creating the conditions that mean people feel more positive about a school or organisation.

Building discretionary effort

Role clarity, leading to consistency and mastery	The extra mile	Openness, transparency and trust, asking first
Personal interest, care and forgiveness		High expectation, leading by example
Ability to inspire, plan and communicate	The extra mile	Focus on the positive, show appreciation
Shared values, purpose and teamwork		Play to people's strengths, be flexible
Support, including manageable workload	The extra mile	Formal and informal career progression
Appropriate challenge and autonomy		Great training, learning and development

Figure 7: Building discretionary effort

It is also important not to fall into the trap of believing these are all about what some might describe as the 'warm and fluffy stuff'! A great culture includes high expectations combined with appropriate challenge and support.

As mentioned in Topic 1, it is also important to remember the greater engagement or discretionary effort doesn't, indeed shouldn't, mean that people are working longer and longer hours. It is about people feeling motivated to work more effectively.

In his book *Drive*, Daniel Pink (2011) gives us a very simple and powerful synthesis of what motivates us at work. All three of his key areas feature in the model above. Based on extensive and respected psychological research, he identifies:

1. Purpose – caring about what we are doing and why it matters.

2. Mastery – the opportunity for us to get really good at something.

3. Autonomy – having the freedom to innovate and personalise what we do.

All three are eminently possible to create in schools, but sometimes leaders can take the first for granted, can change too much too fast, putting the second at risk, or overly specify in detail how people should be doing their jobs, reducing the benefits from the third. The best leaders are either consciously or intuitively tuned into their teams and their context to make sure they get this balance right.

Pink's work also resonates with McGregor's (1960) Theory X and Theory Y model which is summarised in the diagram below.

Theory X	Sphere	Theory Y
Dislike work, find it boring will avoid if we can	ATTITUDE	Need to work, want to take an interest, we can enjoy it
Must be forced or coerced into compliance	DIRECTION	Direct ourselves towards an accepted target
Need to be directed, avoid responsibilty	RESPONSIBILTY	Thrive on responsibility
Motivated by fear, lack of money, lack of job security	MOTIVATION	Motivated by the desire of self-development and to contribute to the world
Little creativity, except when getting around rules	CREATIVITY	Highly creative when given recognition and opportunity

Figure 8: Theory X and Theory Y
McGregor (1960)

Finally, as well as building discretionary effort, a productive culture and climate also has a positive effect on staff retention. As Richard Branson says: 'Train people well enough so they can leave; treat them well enough so that they don't want to'. Given the challenges that never seem to go away when it comes to teacher recruitment in many areas, reducing the requirement to attract new staff by retaining those you already have, makes a great deal of sense.

> ### Key points
> - How would you characterise the culture and climate in your team or organisation?
> - What could you do to build discretionary effort in your context?

Topic 3

Effective leadership development

Leadership and learning are
indispensable to each other.
John F. Kennedy

In writing earlier editions of Leadership Matters, I was really keen to leave it up to you, as the reader, to decide how you access the book, and this approach will still work well with this third edition. You may wish to dip into topics as the need arises, or you may wish to work your way through each of the topics in order. The book has been structured to work either way.

Since then however, lots of schools have been in touch to say they are using it to support their in-school leadership development. Sometimes this has been as simple as running an informal book club where leaders read a topic at a time and discuss it together afterwards, this is often built into existing meeting cycles, which I love! For other colleagues, the book has formed the basis of a more structured in-house leadership learning and development programme. To support both of these approaches, this third edition has been completely reorganised into 40 key leadership topics. New content has also been created to reflect the latest in leadership thinking and a number of companion resources have been added.

Firstly, we have created the Leadership Matters reflective journal, that provides a space for leaders at all levels to structure their thinking, reflections and observations on their successes and areas for growth. Its structure mirrors this book.

Secondly, we have launched a series of 'Leadership Matters in Action' case-study books, written by serving school leaders, which bring to life how schools have taken the Leadership Matters principles and brought them to life in their schools.

Finally, we have updated the Leadership Matters website. This now includes a series of 40 leadership videos that link with both this book and the journal as well as slide packs to go with each topic. These resources sit alongside all the online tools that help you understand yourself as a leader and your context, such as LM Persona, LM 360, LM Style and LM Survey (an easy-to-use way of carrying out pupil, staff and parent surveys). To find out more about these tools there is a summary in Topic 4, or you can visit leadershipmatters.org.uk

If there is one thing that unites all leaders in schools, it's that there is never enough time, so making the structure of these resources as flexible and as simple as possible has been an important part of how the book has been organised. Similarly, for the journal and the videos, the content has been broken down into manageable topics. The videos are bite-sized summaries of the key concepts and models from the book, each between 10 and 15 minutes long. These are designed to be used either by individuals or by groups of colleagues as part of an in-house programme.

What makes great leadership learning and development?

Seeing how more and more schools are starting to make leadership development a collaborative and school-based endeavour is really exciting. No longer is this just about someone going on a one-day leadership course. That's not to say that brilliant programmes like those run by organisations such as Ambition School Leadership or the National College of Education (NCE) don't have their place; they absolutely do. But alongside this, there is nothing more effective that high quality incremental leadership development that is rooted in growing and nurturing strong leadership habits in the workplace. Quite apart from building leadership capacity from within, this approach also helps to develop a common language around leadership within a school or group of schools.

The expert group looking at teacher professional development published its findings in the form of the highly respected *Standard for teachers' professional development* (2016). This got me thinking about what a similar summary might look like for effective leadership development. Here is what I came up with:

1. The approach distinguishes between learning and development, with both included as part of a clear pedagogical framework. It's all very well learning something, but it's only useful if that enables you to develop your practice in a sustainable way.

2. It offers evidence-based leadership knowledge within a carefully constructed curriculum that leaders can then apply within their context.

3. This leadership knowledge sits within a coherent leadership framework. Topic 1 set out the framework we use at Leadership Matters.

4. Learning with and from peers is a key feature of the approach.

5. There is an implicit understanding that leadership habits and skills take time to develop, and the programme length reflects this.

6. An appropriate blend of teaching, mentoring, coaching, personal reflection and goal-setting are an integral part of the approach.

7. Tools that support self-awareness such as personality predisposition and 360-degree feedback are available toward the start of the process. That is why we have created LM Persona, LM Style and LM 360 on the Leadership Matters website.

8. There is an opportunity through carefully curated publications and online resources for participants to personalise their learning. To support this, in addition to LM Video, we have created LM Insight, a part of Leadership Matters that contains links to the very best leadership articles, videos and diagnostic tools available online.

9. There is a focus on the evaluation of impact throughout the process.

10. The overall approach should stretch, support and challenge leaders, leaving them feeling empowered and positive about the future.

Finally, if you are designing and facilitating leadership development sessions yourself, you might wish to reflect on how the 5 Es model below could help you to plan and deliver a great learning and development experience for your colleagues.

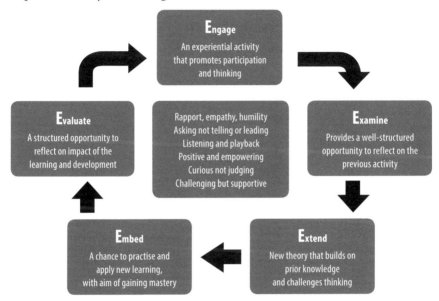

Figure 9: The 5 Es model of learning and development

The boxes around the edge outline suggested key steps for the process. The box in the centre is a useful reminder of the kinds of behaviours from facilitators that will support the very best outcomes for participants.

So, as you continue your leadership journey, may I wish you the very best with whatever you are 'up to' and hope that this book, the journal, the case-studies, the online tools and the videos will add a little something to get you thinking along the way.

Key points

- Is there a particular element you would like to make more of a focus in your leadership development offer?
- In terms of facilitating leadership development sessions, what might be a quick win for you or colleagues?

Topic 4

Leadership Matters resources

If you are willing to be a self-learner,
you will develop yourself.
Lailah Gifty Akita

Resource One: The Leadership Matters journal

If you are one of those schools that is already using this book to support your in-house leadership development, you might be interested in the Leadership Matters Journal. This self-coaching notebook is broken down into a series of 40 topics that match the 40 topics in this book and the 40 videos contained in LM Video (see below).

Each topic then gives school leaders an opportunity to record their reflections on:

- what resonated for them from the topic, in the context of their role
- what steps they commit to take as a result
- what they are going to do to ensure they make these changes happen
- how they will review their success in implementing them.

In other words, the journal provides an opportunity for self- or group-coaching based around the content of this book. In particular, I very much hope it will add a new dimension to schools' and groups of schools' in-house leadership development programmes.

Resource Two: Leadership Matters case-studies

This series of publications, written by school leaders, brings to life how they have taken the Leadership Matters principles and applied them in their schools.

The first of these is *Everyone Succeeds* which charts the journey of Torquay Academy in South-West England, one of the fastest improving schools in the region. It is written by its inspiring principal, Steve Margetts.

Resource Three: Leadership Matters website

The Leadership Matters website offers school leaders the chance to access high quality online tools and videos to support leadership development. These resources can be used by individuals or groups of leaders alongside this book.

Once a school has joined the website, it has one year's unlimited access to all the videos, resources and online tools listed below for any member of staff in the school.

LM Video

This part of the site offers a complete range of short 10- to 15-minute videos based on the 40 topics in this book. These feature me talking through various areas of content, ideas and models from each topic. So if you are using the Leadership Matters book as a resource around which to base a leadership development programme, why not bring it alive with LM Video?

LM Persona

This online tool asks just 20 questions in order to create a detailed predisposition report for any school leader. Based on a Jungian analysis of personality, the tool is designed to help leaders better understand their natural strengths, ways of working and potential areas for growth. As I argue in Section A of the book, great leadership starts with individuals knowing themselves well. LM Persona can help school leaders have a greater insight into their leadership predispositions.

LM 360

This tool gives school leaders the chance to rate themselves against 40 key leadership competencies linked to the content of this book. It also allows leaders to identify up to six people from whom they would like to seek similar feedback. In addition, there is an opportunity for colleagues to give short written feedback on three areas of strength and a possible area for growth. All this feedback is then anonymously collated and automatically emailed back to the school leader concerned. The report also includes a brief analysis of the data, highlighting six areas of strength for the individual and some practical advice on three possible areas for growth, all linking back to one or more of the 40 Leadership Matters topics.

LM Style

All of us have leadership styles we prefer to use. This simple tool helps identify which styles we are likely to use more often and those we may tend to neglect. Knowing the latter can be useful for school leaders, as all leadership styles are needed at some time or other. Based around Daniel Goleman's model (2000), the tool links with Topic 37 in both the book and LM Video.

LM Survey

Many schools already seek the views of parents, pupils and staff about how well they think their school is doing, but these can be very time consuming or expensive to undertake. LM Survey is a great way to take your school's temperature. In just one click, you can create a bespoke link that can be sent out to pupils, staff or parents, which allows them to answer a number of pre-set questions. You can also add in your own questions or delete any of the standard questions before the link is sent out. LM Survey can be repeated as many times as you want, so can be used by specific year groups of pupils or parents or different groups of staff.

LM Team

This fully automated tool allows members of any team in your school to gather views on how effectively that team is working. Most often used by senior teams, it asks a series of questions that are converted into a visual representation of the team's effectiveness. The tool is based on the team development model outlined in Topic 25.

LM Present

These are bespoke slide packs to go with each of the 40 topics on LM Video. Each slide pack has the hyperlinks to any relevant LM Video clips embedded within them. For each slide pack there is also a short PDF that offers advice on using the resource, should you find this useful.

LM Insight

This part of the Leadership Matters website contains links to the very best leadership articles, videos and diagnostic tools available online. While these are all open-source resources, the idea of LM Insight is to save school leaders time by curating all these great resources into one easy-to-access place, organised in line with the structure of the book.

LM Books

This is a member benefit that allows schools to buy multiple copies of Leadership Matters and other selected John Catt publications at significantly discounted prices.

LM Template

This is a collection of simple leadership templates for schools to download and use. For example, there is a Word version of the 'checklist for change' document mentioned in Topic 34.

LM People

This part of the website enables anyone to make contact with Leadership Matters recommended coaches, trainers and keynote speakers. Finding people you know you can trust in these important areas can sometimes be difficult. Leadership Matters doesn't benefit financially from signposting these individuals, it's just another way we like to support schools with creating high quality leadership development opportunities.

LM Meet

Free regional leadership development days hosted around the country by Leadership Matters ambassadors and authors. It's a chance for Leadership Matters members to share ideas and experiences with one another as well as hear some of the Leadership Matters content brought alive by the creators of the resources.

Unlimited access to all the tools listed above is available for one single membership fee per school. To find out more, visit leadershipmatters.org.uk

Using 360 feedback

Of all these resources, there is one that requires careful handling: LM 360. This type of feedback can be incredibly powerful, but at the same time if it is used badly it can have a negative impact on a leader's development.

Here are my top tips for using LM 360 successfully:

- It's usually better to use 360 feedback for leadership development rather than performance management or appraisal. It needs to be non-threatening and supportive.
- Keep individuals in control of the process. Let them choose who to ask for feedback. Let them have time to process and interpret their feedback.
- Keep the focus on behaviours and actions not the person's self-concept.
- Ensure there is an appropriate balance of areas of strength as well as areas for growth.
- Offer a coaching approach alongside feedback (an independent coach or a line manager).
- Keep development points to an absolute minimum. Leadership development is all about changing habits through the deliberate practice of one or two areas at a time.
- Make these performance goals specific, practical and achievable.
- It's best not to provide comparative data with others who may be using the same feedback tool. This takes away the focus on personal growth and adds a competitive element that can cause some individuals to become defensive or feel threatened.
- Allow individuals to repeat the feedback process at appropriate intervals so improvements can be acknowledged and celebrated.
- Help individuals to develop a follow-up action plan, with practical support that focuses on the specific goals identified.
- Support individuals to make the most of their feedback by remaining curious and interested rather than judgemental. This builds trust and can lead to challenging yet supportive conversations.

Key points

- Are there any new elements of the Leadership Matters offer that you would like to start using?
- Would using 360 feedback be a useful addition to your provision, or is there anything about the way you use 360 feedback you would like to change?

Section A

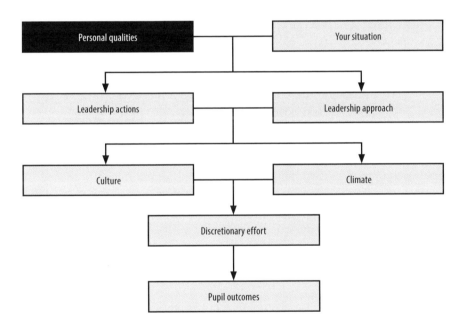

Personal qualities

Leaders come in many forms, with many styles and diverse qualities. There are quiet leaders and leaders one can hear in the next county. Some find strength in eloquence, some in judgment, some in courage.

John W. Gardner

For as long as I can remember, I have read about the importance of leaders knowing themselves. I have to admit that it was only toward the end of my second headship, after more than 15 years in senior leadership roles, that I began to take this sentiment seriously. If I am honest, it always sounded like the sort of thing someone who wasn't actually in a leadership position might say. Something of theoretical interest but of little practical relevance.

As a school leader, what mattered to me was working out the right thing to do and getting everyone doing it to a high standard. So I understood the need to assess a situation, and I appreciated the importance of developing strategy. I knew it mattered to get others on board and excited about what we wanted to achieve. I knew it was important to monitor progress and outcomes closely to see how we were doing.

But what I didn't allow for were my own predispositions in all of that. All of us respond to situations in different ways, both emotionally and rationally. We bring all sorts of preconceptions and predispositions to situations. We are more or less able to accurately read the emotions of others or even to manage our own if we are able recognise them. All of which makes us more or less able to make good decisions or form effective relationships with others.

I can recall many situations when, for whatever reason, things didn't always work out the way I had hoped. When I look back on my first headship, my default reaction was usually to blame, not to try to find out why something hadn't worked. This was often followed by trying, usually single-handedly, to find a solution and then pretty much impose it on everyone else. Alongside this, I was quick to make judgements about others' competence, and sometimes people decided it was best to leave the school. Of course, in many cases this was the right thing. Great schools, to use Jim Collins' analogy in *Good to Great* (2001), are good at getting the right people on the bus and the wrong people off. As a leader at any level, you need to be clear about the standards you expect and hold others to account, but I think I was too quick to act in some of those situations. I am naturally predisposed to take swift and decisive action without always taking the time to think something through. It is a preference I am still working to manage; a habit I am still changing.

What can the experts tell about all this? Topic 5 explores Daniel Goleman's emotional intelligence model (2000). Topic 6 on self-awareness looks at two key theories:

- Ingram and Luft's Johari window (1955)
- Jung's view of personality predisposition

I am not a psychologist. But what I share in Topic 6 are my practical reflections on these models. Why understanding one's own predispositions means, as a school leader, you will be able to make better decisions, manage relationships more effectively and be better placed to ensure great delivery.

Sharing your predispositions with others can also be powerful. If colleagues know the things you are good at and enjoy doing, the whole team can benefit from those strengths. If there are things that energise you, let others know. Conversely, if there are particular behaviours that de-motivate or irritate you, let others know these too. Finally, if there are particular predispositions that you are working to manage more effectively, it can be helpful to tell colleagues. Not only can they give you feedback when you are doing well on these, which is helpful in itself, they can also give a gentle reminder when you are not!

The remaining two topics in this part of the book focus on key personal qualities that appear to underpin great school leadership at all levels. Topic 7 examines the importance of courage and resilience, and Topic 8 reminds us that great leaders show humility. They are very good at their job and achieve great things for the pupils they serve, but never forget it is a team effort.

Topic 5
Emotional intelligence

I think self-awareness is probably
the most important thing towards
becoming a champion.
Billie Jean King

The turn of the century saw the emergence of the concept of emotional intelligence (EQ). Setting aside the debate about whether this is an intelligence at all, or simply a set of personal competences, in his seminal article for the Harvard Business Review, *Leadership that gets results* (2000), Daniel Goleman's model brought the idea to international prominence. He suggests that a leader's EQ is likely to be a much more important indicator of their effectiveness than their intelligence (IQ). Of course, IQ is important, but Goleman argues that the thing that distinguishes standout performance is much more likely to be EQ. This makes a lot of sense to me. In schools we need to deliver through others if we are to deliver great outcomes for pupils. We can't do everything ourselves, so building great relationships is critical. As a former busy school leader, the strength of Goleman's model is also its simplicity. He identified just four key domains for emotional intelligence, which are set out in the Figure 10.

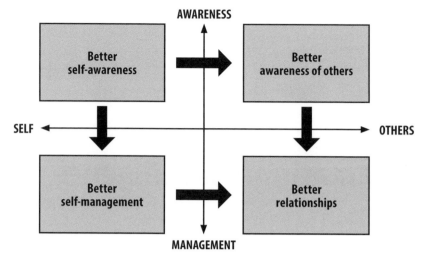

Figure 10: A model of emotional intelligence
Daniel Goleman

As the model summarises, Goleman believes emotional intelligence begins with better self-awareness. This in turn supports one's awareness of others and provides an opportunity for you to manage your own emotions. Together, the combination of these two provide the basis by which one is able to build better relationships. Going right back to the start of this part of the book, it is why self-awareness in leaders matters so much, as it pretty much defines one's ability to build relationships with others, which is critical for any leader.

Understanding your emotional responses
While colleagues, parents and pupils might detect external signs of your behaviour in a difficult conversation, none will usually be able to identify how you are feeling inside. A difficult discussion with a parent whose child might require the support of social services, or a member of staff who is not following a departmental or school marking policy will arouse a range of emotions. Similarly, how are you likely to respond if you are told you are going to need to make significant budget cuts or need to make colleagues redundant?

These emotional responses are natural and not a sign of vulnerability. If you can identify these and know what kinds of situations trigger stress or emotional responses in you, then you have a better chance of remaining in control of a situation. Being able to identify situations that arouse strong emotions means you can identify and interpret those emotions. It also allows you to remain more objective. A powerful strategy can be to reflect on a situation by imagining yourself stepping outside your body and viewing your situation objectively. What would you tell yourself to do?

Role-modelling self-awareness

This works at two levels. Ideally, you want to build a culture and climate in your own team where self-awareness is valued and practised. It can be incredibly powerful for your team to see you role modelling being self-aware or acting as the 'learning-centred leader'. One of the most striking ways to do this is for you to admit that you do not know the answer to something, or that you need the support of your team to solve a problem. This shows others that continuous learning and reflection is nothing to be ashamed of and is an important part of developing as a leader.

If you are feeling confident, you might even admit a development area or a challenge and invite feedback or ideas from colleagues. In The Advantage, (2014) Lencioni describes a range of team exercises that use the sharing of feedback as a mechanism for building trust and establishing a culture of reflection. For example, you might invite your team to give you feedback on how you could have handled a situation differently. By putting yourself in the position of receiving feedback, you powerfully model that you value reflection and self-awareness.

Your own EQ profile

If you are interested in finding out more about your strengths in each of the four domains Goleman identified, you can access an online tool via the LM Insight section of the Leadership Matters website at leadershipmatters.org.uk

The rest of this topic outlines some practical ways you can build your competence in each area.

Better self-awareness

- Ask others about your strengths and weaknesses, including using 360 feedback, if this is possible.
- Become more finely attuned to physical reactions you have in certain situations and learn to recognise them.
- Keep a diary of your emotional shifts.
- Notice how you react in each case. What do you think? Are there any physical responses? What would others see you do?
- If you notice an emotional reaction in yourself, try to identify the cause.
- Know your emotional triggers. You can then respond in a purposeful controlled way, rather than automatically.

Better awareness of others

- Remember that when it comes to expressing emotions, 7% of communication is what is said; 38% through tone of voice and 55% through body-language.
- Watch for mirroring of body-language in others.
- Watch TV programmes or films with the sound turned down and see what you observe.
- Ask more open questions. Be neutral in the way you ask them so people say what they really think.
- Listen more closely for deep understanding.
- Look for the way people behave in meetings, not just what they say.
- Look for what's not being said.
- Avoid finishing others' sentences.
- Check for understanding.

Better self-management

- This is not about controlling emotions but managing your response most productively.
- Take responsibility for your emotions. You create them, not others.

- Do something that requires you to think rationally.
- Have letters or emails about your successes that you can read when you feel like you have lost your confidence.
- Learn to reflect in the moment. Use this thinking time to detach yourself from the emotion.

Better relationships

- Affirm throughout a conversation, especially when not talking.
- Paraphrase and summarise. Show you have listened.
- Under promise and over deliver.
- Find out what matters to other people. Are they, for example, motivated by moral purpose, or the logic of an argument, or your passion or just in gaining power and influence?
- Be gently proactive in maintaining communication. Don't wait for them.
- Praise in writing. Challenge face-to-face.
- Talk less than you listen.

Key points

- Have you considered your strengths and potential areas for growth in relation to EQ?
- Might it be useful to visit the diagnostic tool accessible via the Leadership Matters website?
- Where might you want to focus on building your EQ competence and what are you going to do?

Topic 6

Self-awareness and predisposition

Predisposition is not predestination.
William Landay

'Know thyself' was written on the forecourt of the Temple of Apollo at Delphi as a message to the philosophers, statesmen and law-givers who laid the foundation for western culture. It is one of the greatest challenges for every leader: to know their strengths and development areas, to know what arouses strong emotions in themselves and how to manage those feelings.

If you are a middle leader, stepping into a leadership role for the first time, your voyage of self-discovery is usually faster than it will be at any other point in your career. You are learning all the time, taking on new responsibilities, managing up and down, and often still have a pretty full timetable and little time to step back and reflect.

Your experiences and strengths as a teacher helped you reach your middle leadership position, and while you need to retain those strengths in your new role, you are now exposing yourself to new challenges which will create new development areas. As a senior leader, managing a new middle leader, this is where you can really add value. You can help them identify their new development areas and support them, through mentoring and coaching, to build their skills in these areas. You can also help them reflect on how they are progressing.

But for senior leaders, too, the journey to self-awareness never ends. As I mentioned earlier, it took rather too long for me to realise the potential and power of strong self-awareness.

Knowing yourself

There are a number of ways you can get to know yourself better. One way of course, is to build honest and open relationships so people just say it to you as it is! But this isn't always easy to do, particularly when it comes to getting feedback from people from within your team. One way round this is for you to take part in a more structured 360 feedback survey. There are a number of variations on how a 360 survey can be conducted, but they are basically designed to allow you to reflect on your own strengths and areas for development and then see how they align with the perceptions of around five other colleagues. This feedback will usually come from a range of individuals: those who are more senior than you, your peers and those who are part of your team. In other words, they represent a 360 view.

While these are starting to become a little more commonplace than they were a few years ago, we are a long way from all middle and senior leaders viewing 360 survey tools as a routine part of the feedback they should expect to receive to support their development. Part of the reason for this is that it has either been too expensive or too time-consuming to operate 360 surveys for all leaders in a school or group of schools. However, there are a number of online options that schools can consider, some of which represent excellent value. At Leadership Matters, we have created our own anonymous and fully automated survey called LM 360, with 40 questions structured around the leadership model underpinning this book, as well as the opportunity to offer other feedback on personal strengths and potential areas for growth.

You might also consider using one of the many online personality tools available to increase self-awareness. A popular example is the Myers-Briggs Type Indicator (MBTI) that gives an indication of behavioural preferences in four opposing dichotomies. At Leadership Matters we have developed an online tool that is also based on a Jungian model of personality type, called LM Persona. As with any of these personality tools, it is important not to use the outcome of any process to help you justify to yourself or others why you can't do certain things. For example, someone who likes leaving things to the last minute and prefers to keep things open and flexible (which can be a strength in certain situations) shouldn't allow this to be a reason why they can't be more planned and organised. Just like writing with your other hand, it is just a bit more difficult and takes more deliberate practice.

It's also worth reflecting on the best way to use any particular personality tool. For me, we have to accept that all tools will have their limitations. Take MBTI, for example. It is one of the most commonly used personality instruments right across the globe. Yet there are those that challenge whether there is sufficient evidence to support the efficacy of the instrument itself. I suspect arguments about this and other tools will always be with us. It seems to me that a sensible and pragmatic approach to using any tool might be to follow these steps:

1. Take part in the review process.

2. Look at what emerges.

3. Decide for oneself what is helpful and just focus on that.

In other words, use a tool to help shed a little light on oneself and then take it from there, rather than becoming fixated on one's personality type. Taking this approach focuses on what really matters: using such tools to support self-reflection and personal development.

What neuroscience teaches us

Recent research into how the brain works has also given us much greater insight into how we can develop new skills, so long as we do indeed practise them deliberately and persistently. The brain has now been proven to demonstrate what is known as neuro-plasticity – the ability to create and secure new neural pathways as a result of repeated practice. For us as school leaders, the good news is that we really can change our leadership habits. By identifying areas for growth and focusing on them, we can improve our effectiveness. But there would appear to be a limit on the number of habits we can change at any one time. While we are all different in the extent to which this applies, we all need to focus on developing a small number of skills or habits at any given moment. To do otherwise is to risk not actually achieving any of the goals we have set ourselves.

Using personality predisposition tools and 360 feedback will allow you to reflect on your own strengths and areas for growth, as well as compare your own perceptions with those of your colleagues. This may confirm what you knew already or, more helpfully, tell you something you didn't know. The Johari window (Luft and Ingham, 1955) is a model that groups these areas into four categories:

1. *Open*, which are those known by you and others.

2. *Hidden*, which are known by you but which you do not reveal to others.

3. *Blind spot*, which are those others know about you, but you do not know about yourself.

4. *Unknown* which are those that are not known to you or others.

The unknown areas are the hardest to discover and, apart from using 360 feedback, often the best way to find these is when you put yourself in new or particularly challenging situations, when more concealed emotions are often heightened and become more evident.

	Known to self	Not known to self
Known to others	**OPEN**	**BLIND SPOT**
Not known to others	**HIDDEN**	**UNKNOWN**

Figure 11: The Johari window
Luft and Ingham (1955)

Consistent review

Whatever your leadership role, making time to regularly review your own performance is a useful habit to develop.

There are four ways you can do this:

- Make the time to reflect – do you systematically and regularly make time to think about the effectiveness of your leadership practice?
- Asking for feedback – do you make a point of asking for feedback from colleagues, parents, pupils and peers?
- Practise mindfulness – what strategies do you use to relax and create the mental space for you to reflect?
- Critical friend – who do you speak to beyond your line manager in order to process your thoughts and ideas and get an external perspective on your challenges? Might you benefit from having a coach, particularly if you are facing an exciting but slightly daunting leadership transition?

Key points

- Do you know your own predispositions as a leader?
- Do you play to your strengths?
- Are there any areas you know you need to keep in mind and try to manage more effectively as they have the potential to limit your effectiveness?
- How can others help you achieve this?

Topic 7

Courage and resilience

Anyone can hold the helm
when the sea is calm.
Publilius Syrus

Leadership at any level in a school brings with it many challenges. This topic looks at the importance of having the courage to do the right thing and to keep going.

The challenges of middle leadership

If you are a middle leader, your job is undoubtedly one of the most pressurised in school. While senior leaders are in control of whole-school strategy and direction, as a middle leader, you sit at the heart of the school leadership team managing up, down and across, implementing the changes that come from above and managing the situations which arise below you. The role of middle leaders is also shifting, demanding more autonomy and accountability, which makes resilience and courage more important than ever before.

Changes stemming from government policies can often mean you are at the heart of implementing regular change coming from outside your school. You are faced with more ambiguity, inconsistency and change from above and outside, making long-term decisions harder to reach, and while in theory you may have more autonomy, it often doesn't feel like that. Technology has removed physical barriers, so you can be reached anywhere, anytime and do not have the time and space to think.

Senior leadership

It might seem obvious, but as a senior leader, while the potential impact of your work and the decisions you make can be much greater, so too is the potential for pressure and worry. Decisions you take have bigger implications for you personally if things go wrong, the school, your staff and, most importantly, your pupils. The pressure of public accountability, particularly for heads and system leaders, is significant. As with middle leadership, external pressures can be intense. It can sometimes feel like expectations keep rising, finding great teachers gets harder and there are never enough resources to do what you really believe needs to be done.

Added to this is the pressure that comes from dealing with unplanned and sometimes shocking events that can hit you out of the blue. I remember talking to one head a few years ago who described how she had to lead her school into an inspection in the same week that a member of her staff had committed suicide following a school-related incident. In such circumstances, the best leaders seem to draw on an indescribable source of inspiration and energy that lies deep within their psyche. In this case, the head concerned led her school to its first ever outstanding judgement.

The unshakeable conviction and determination to do what it takes in order to do the right thing for the school and the young people that it serves seems to be at the heart of the drive and passion that circumstances like this bring forth from these outstanding leaders.

So what is it that great leaders at all levels do which makes a difference?

Managing your emotions

In order to stay strong for your team, you have to stay strong yourself, which means managing your emotions, as we saw in Topic 5. Emotions are not a sign of weakness; in fact, recognising and identifying how you are feeling is a real strength. Different situations make different people feel stressed. Do you know what situations make you feel stressed? Do you know what makes you worry or feel anxious? The important thing is to recognise your emotions but not be governed by them.

If you recognise your emotions then you probably know how to manage them. Maybe when you feel stressed or worried you need to talk to someone you trust to get a different perspective. Maybe you need to create some personal space to think through the problem. Maybe you need to go for a run or do something different to clear your head.

Some questions to ask yourself might include:

- How do I feel?
- Why do I feel that way (for example a recent event, or criticism)?
- Is this something that normally triggers an emotional response?
- What would I tell myself to do if I were observing from outside?

Turning negativity into positivity

In the moments of highest pressure and negative criticism you have two choices: you can either let the criticism build into a negative spiral, or you can use it as an opportunity to respond positively and build support. If you can soak up the criticism, show you are listening, prove to others that you want to adapt, improve and learn, then you can turn negative situations into positive ones. The game is only over if you give up.

Put yourself in the position of the person giving feedback or criticism. Often they may just want to voice frustration, they may be under pressure themselves which they are projecting, or they may really care and only sound negative because they want things to be better. Either way, you cannot lose if you respond positively. If you can tap into why they are behaving the way they are then you can use their feedback to build support.

Some questions you may want to ask:

- How are they behaving (anger, frustration, or commitment)?
- What are they saying (do they want improvement, change, or vindication)?
- What is behind the words (influence, affirmation, or veiled support)?
- What do they want to hear (apology, commitment to change, or that they are right)?

Staying optimistic

If you can manage yourself and not let the external criticism get on top of you, then the next group to focus on is your team. Jon Coles, my former boss at United Learning and a former senior director at the Department for Education, talks about leaders needing to exhibit *unwarranted optimism*. Staff look to leaders in school for reassurance when things are difficult. They need to see leaders being optimistic, however hard this is to do, to make them feel secure in difficult or uncertain circumstances.

Here are some practical ways in which this can be achieved:

- Recognising and celebrating small successes to build momentum and positivity in the team.
- Praising the team to keep them positive, you will find this makes you more positive too.
- Communicating so that others hear your voice regularly and you control the flow of information and messages.
- Being authentic and honest so they feel they can trust you to deliver a tough message when it is required.
- Copying role models – when you are feeling vulnerable, copy the behaviour of others who appear in control.
- Communicating your vision – your vision will inspire the team and remind them about the big picture and the reasons behind what you are doing.

Learning and improving from criticism

The first thing about criticism is to try not to analyse it in the moment. Often it is hard to be objective about criticism and pressure when you are receiving it because emotions, sensitivities and fears are heightened. If you feel like you want to give feedback or find yourself using language of blame or fault, then it may not be the right time to analyse. The heat of the moment is not the time to start saying 'if only we had done this…'

Keep a log of the feedback, problems and actions so that you can look back once the crisis has passed and everyone has found something to be positive about. You are then in a safe space to look back and analyse what has happened. Let everyone share their perspectives and what they would do, finding time and space to listen and digest the different information you are hearing. Make sure that any face-to-face conversations are held in private and not in public if you need to have tough conversations.

Finally, make sure everyone commits to the changes you want to make. Allowing them to feed in will be critical, but make sure they know you are still committed, motivated and certain that the team can succeed moving forward.

Keeping going

Peter Matthews in his Ofsted publication, *Twelve outstanding secondary schools* (2009) talks about the 'tireless energy' that leaders in the schools he studied demonstrated. Their schools didn't become outstanding overnight. It was the culmination of hard work over a significant period of time. The building of this momentum is the result of ongoing determination and a rigorous focus on the school's core business. For school leaders, the implication is very clear: running a successful school takes a huge amount of hard work! Not just because it is important that school leaders need to be seen to be leading by example, but also because there appears to be almost no other way. Just when you have one thing sorted, something else crops up. There is always something else to do.

None of the heads I have met in the last few years give the impression that their workload had diminished in any way. In fact the reverse is probably true.

Taking calculated risks

The last area this topic relates to is the importance of school leaders taking risks. This takes courage in itself, not that these risks won't have been carefully considered before they are taken. To take one example, giving relatively junior members of staff key roles within a school can easily backfire. Yet this approach can have a major impact by helping create a culture where people learn on the job and develop themselves, becoming self-motivated and self-disciplined. It also provides a clear sense that the leadership of the school values the people that work there, which builds a positive climate. Together, taking these risks and having the courage to believe in colleagues builds momentum and leadership capacity, and enhances trust.

The very best leaders also have the courage to take risks about what they are *not* to going to do. Jim Collins' 'hedgehog concept' is all about keeping the focus on what an institution knows it does well and is its core business. Deciding not to undertake certain activities, even when all around them are, takes courage. I remember as a head, a few years ago now, when we decided our school would not engage with the new Diploma qualification. We just weren't convinced it was going to work in practice. This was most definitely a risky strategy, as the government had set a date when all schools needed to provide their pupils with access to the range of Diploma qualifications. But it was a calculated risk and one based upon doing what we thought was right for our pupils. In the end, the qualification wasn't popular with pupils, parents and schools nationwide and the initiative folded.

The excellent NCSL publication *A model of urban leadership in challenging urban environments* (2004) describes how the best leaders show courage by:

- standing up for their beliefs and defending them in the face of opposition and entrenched interests
- doing the right thing rather than taking the easy option, despite the possible risks and complications
- taking calculated risks, where appropriate, to improve provision for pupils.

One head once told me how his school had decided to create a two-year KS3 well before anyone else had done this. Yet four years later, with the abolition of KS3 SATs, many schools decided to follow suit. The same school also decided to do away with tutor groups and tutorial time in favour of dedicated one-to-one coaching for pupils provided by all the adults working at the school. For this trailblazing school, both decisions were calculated risks that took courage, but both ultimately contributed to the school gaining its first outstanding judgement that year. Of course, these decisions must be seen in the light of a particular context. For many, the idea of a two-year KS3 only results in a narrower curriculum than many pupils ought to have access to.

In a wider context, one leader of a multi-academy trust I know decided with senor colleagues a few years ago that they would only take new schools into their trust if they were within a close geographical area, to allow for meaningful collaboration and the flexible deployment of staff. At that time, government policy was to grow the academies movement as fast as possible, and the trust was risking losing government support because of its stance. In the end, however, time has shown this approach to growth to have been a successful strategy and indeed government policy has changed to reflect this.

A model for resilience

One useful model for considering the key elements of resilience has been developed by an organisation called Robertson Cooper. They believe there are four key dimensions to resilience, as shown in the diagram below.

CONFIDENCE
1. Self-belief
2. Coping with stressful situations
3. Right balance of positive and negative emotions

SOCIAL SUPPORT
1. Good relationship with others
2. Willingness to seek support
3. Knowing when to draw on the support

ADAPTABILITY
1. Able to cope with change, particularly when imposed
2. Flexible when needed
3. Can recover quickly in such situations

PURPOSEFULNESS
1. Clear sense of purpose in role
2. Strong values, drive and direction
3. Achieve in the face of setbacks

Figure 12: A model for resilience
Adapted from Robertson Cooper

If you are interested in finding out more about your strengths in each of these areas, you can access an online diagnostic tool via the LM Insight section of the Leadership Matters website at leadershipmatters.org.uk

Key points

- How good are you at appreciating and managing your emotions?
- Are you able to keep optimistic, even in the most difficult circumstances?
- Do you usually learn from your mistakes?
- Are you good at taking those difficult decisions or occasionally admitting publicly when you are wrong?
- Do you have the courage to take calculated risks, even if this sometimes involves going out on a limb?
- What are your strengths and potential areas for growth in the resilience model shared in this topic?

Topic 8

Humility

Humility is not thinking less of yourself;
it's thinking of yourself less.
C. S. Lewis

When thinking about the structure of this book, it was tempting to include the contents of this short topic in with one of the others. However, while this part of the book makes a simple point that doesn't take a huge amount of explaining, to have included it as part of another topic would have undermined its importance.

When Jim Collins in his book *Good to Great* (2001) looked at the companies that he judged had made the move from good to great, he discovered something very interesting about the leaders of those companies. Unsurprisingly, all of them were very ambitious. However, this ambition was not focused on their own achievements but on being ambitious for their organisation. They were, in fact, very modest about their own personal achievements. When they talked about their companies, it was more as if their successes were as a result of a huge team effort of which they had the privilege to be at the helm.

The power of humility

When I was responsible for running the London Challenge *Good to Great* programme, as the head of a school that was judged 'good' at the time, we used to invite heads from schools that had been judged 'outstanding' three or four times to come and talk to us about their journeys. As we listened to these successful school leaders at our conferences, exactly the same phenomenon that Jim Collins identified emerged strongly. The heads all extolled the virtues of their staff, pupils and the support they have received from the families in their community. Of course, they acknowledged the importance of their own personal leadership and their drive for continuous improvement, but they were all modest about their achievements, wanting always to give the credit to others rather than to themselves.

In some ways, this finding isn't too surprising. After all, this is exactly the type of leadership that will build trust among staff and help people to develop themselves and learn in the workplace. It will also encourage an open, honest and transparent environment where leaders have the emotional intelligence and self-awareness to recognise the importance of celebrating the achievements of everyone, while at the same time keeping the focus on performance and continuous improvement.

But the definition of humility here is not about false modesty, these leaders have a grounded and honest sense of who has achieved what. They are confident about their own abilities and don't need to prove themselves to others by advertising their own achievements.

Respecting uncertainty

But as Michael Fullan points out in *The six secrets of change* (2008) there is another reason why effective leaders remain humble. Schools are no different from any other organisation in that they operate within an incredibly complex environment. For example, how we should use new technologies such as social networking to support learning, what we know about how the brain works, the challenges of recruiting teachers and the rapid changes to population demographics, all present leaders of our schools with an ever-changing landscape.

Any leader who is not humbled by the complexities of such an environment and who doesn't recognise the need to keep learning and keep up to speed with the developments around them is unlikely to remain as a leader in a high performing school.

Building momentum, loyalty and trust

There is also clear evidence that leaders who don't see themselves as being above certain types of work have a strong impact on building momentum. Peter Matthews was clear in his study of *Twelve outstanding schools* (2009) that the heads and other school leaders, however senior, all recognised the importance of being 'hands on'. The school leaders who are prepared to demonstrate that they have both the ability and willingness to tackle the tasks that they expect everyone else to do not only gain huge personal respect, but they help create the kind of alignment that builds organisational momentum.

This is humility in a different sense. It is making a clear statement that a leader is no better than anyone else. That they understand they are part of a team where everyone is an essential part of that team and where the individual role that each person plays is critical to the success of the whole school.

Demonstrating the willingness to carry out any role also builds trust, particularly when taking the time to join with others in what might be seen as more menial tasks such as putting out the chairs for assembly, serving school lunches when they are short staffed or signing in parents at a parents' evening. Where such action is linked with small acts of kindness, they are even more powerful. For example, when a leader offers to do duty or take a register for a colleague who just needs some time alone for a moment, the loyalty which that simple act buys will inevitably be multiplied ten times over.

A focus on the school, not the leader

In drawing this topic to a close, it is important to remember that I am not saying the best leaders are not ambitious, competitive or driven. They are absolutely focused on achieving the best they can for their teams and their schools or group of schools. What sets the leaders in the best organisations apart is that the ambition is for the school or organisation itself, not for them as an individual.

This links back to the importance of moral purpose. The most successful leaders want the best for their pupils. Of course, it is important that their work is enjoyable, fun and personally rewarding. But the main motivator is the success of the organisation as a whole, not for them as an individual leader.

Key points

- Do you give credit to others for the success of your team or school(s)?
- Are you emotionally self-aware? If yes, how do you know?
- Are you prepared to lead by example in any role and do not portray yourself as being too important to do certain types of work?
- Are you always keen to learn more and keep improving?

Section B

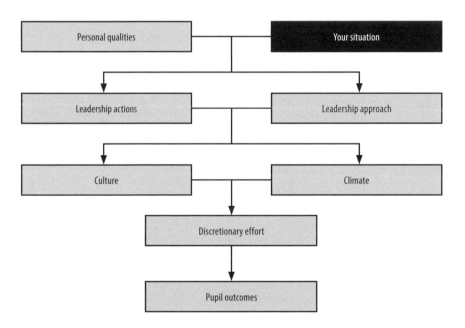

Your situation

Understanding context is worth 80 IQ points.
Alan Kay

Section A of this book was about the importance of taking time to properly understand your own predispositions and proactively take steps to play to your strengths as well as manage both your emotions and your habits in those areas that might reduce your effectiveness as a leader. You may remember this was something, with hindsight, that I think appreciated rather late in my own development as a leader!

This next section of the book is all about the other half of this equation. Not your internal world that has been our focus so far, but the external world within which you lead. This could be a part of your school, the whole school or even a group of schools, depending on your role, but crucially, before you decide what you need to focus on as a leader, or how you might go about implementing these priorities, you need to understand your situation properly.

At the highest level, this breaks down into the two Ps: performance and people. Firstly, what is the effectiveness of your area of responsibility or the school you lead? Where are you on your journey? In other words, how's the performance? Topics 9 and 10 look at this in more detail. The focus of topics 10 and 11, however, is on your understanding of the people you are working with.

Topic 9

Context

*A few observations and much reasoning
lead to error; many observations
and a little reasoning to truth.*
Alexis Carrel

Understanding your context properly is crucial before you decide upon your priorities for action and approach to implementation. How well do you know your operating context, whether that is a phase, curriculum area or pastoral team within a school, a school itself or a group of schools? Working out your strategy has to begin with where you are and what you need to do to get to where you want to go.

Performance data can tell you a lot about your context, particularly when the data is benchmarked against similar schools and national averages. But there are many other sources of evidence that you may want to take into account, as performance data alone can sometimes present quite a narrow snapshot of context.

Many schools use anonymous survey or questionnaire data to identify strengths and areas for development. The majority of the tools available provide useful data on national averages that enable you to benchmark your current position. At Leadership Matters, we have developed a tool we call LM Survey that provides powerful feedback from three key stakeholder groups: pupils, parents and staff. The latter, of course, gives you a great insight into how levels of discretionary effort are improving over time.

But there is also no substitute for talking to as many people as you can, at every opportunity, and in a way that makes people feel at ease and free to say what they really think, which is a skill in itself! Apart from gleaning useful information, spending time talking to colleagues can also do a lot to increase engagement and discretionary effort, so long as people feel that it has been a genuine process. I know a number of heads that interviewed every single member of staff when they joined their school to find out what was working well and what would make the school even better. The impact on staff was universally positive – everyone likes to feel they have been heard. I even know one head who, after more than 15 years of headship in the same school, still meets with every member of the teaching and support staff every single year!

Combining your evidence

As you will be well aware, the more you can triangulate your evidence, the more accurate the picture you can create of where you are on your journey. Topic 10 looks at monitoring and data in more detail. Using pupil progress data, broken down to pupil sub-groups, phases or curriculum areas and linking this to other evidence from lesson observations, learning walks and pupil voice, you can start to gain a much more reliable notion of the key measure we all care about most: the impact of teaching over time.

We all know the teachers that can turn on a good lesson when they are being observed. But it is highly debatable whether that gives an indication of the typicality of their teaching, or when combined with the quality of feedback, the typicality of pupil progress. And even if it did, Michael Strong's 2011 work on lesson observation calls into question the reliability of grading single lessons in this way.

| 1st rater gives | % | Probability that 2nd rater disagrees | |
		Best case r = 0.7	Worst case r = 0.24
Outstanding	12%	51%	78%
Good	55%	31%	43%
Req. Impr.	29%	46%	64%
Inadequate	4%	62%	90%
Overall		**39%**	**55%**

Percentages based on simulations

Figure 13: Reliability of lesson observations

Adapted by Rob Coe based on the work of Michael Strong (2003)

As the table above shows, there is a significant chance that two observations of the same lesson can reach a different conclusion as to the overall lesson grade.

The ladder of inference

One of the reasons different individuals may come to different conclusions about the quality of the same lesson, despite using exactly the same rubric, is that we all bring our own experiences and subconscious prejudices to bear. These inevitably have an impact on how we interpret what we observe. We have a tendency to be selective when absorbing the information in front of us and on the basis of this partial picture, we create a set of assumptions about the world around us. These assumptions lead to us drawing conclusions about situations and ultimately creating a set of beliefs. These in turn feed back down into how we select data; usually that which reinforces our view of the world. In addition, our beliefs will tend to influence the actions we take, and this in turn lead us to turn our attention to certain sets of data, thus re-starting the whole process. This phenomenon is known as the ladder of inference and is summarised in Figure 14.

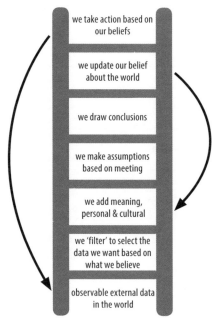

Figure 14: The ladder of inference
Argyris and Senge (1970)

Put simply, school leaders are no different from anyone else – we are always at risk of making assumptions and jumping to conclusions. Developing the habit of taking time to properly understand situations, often through asking open questions and giving consideration to as wide a range of data and information as possible, can make a big difference to one's understanding of a situation. Linked to this, inviting others to challenge our own perspectives, and thanking them when they do, is also an important habit in a leader. If others are afraid to challenge us as leaders, we run the risk of perpetuating our view of the world, which can lead to us losing touch with the reality of situations.

The composite view of context

So as well as understanding those around you, it is also critical to be clear about your wider context, taking into account as many sources of data and information as you can. Whatever level of leadership you are operating at, this will enable you to be even more effective at deciding what you need to do and how to go about doing it.

Sir David Carter, who was the National Schools Commissioner for England, has come up with a simple yet highly effective way to think about a school's context on its journey to becoming great. Figure 15 sets out his model.

Figure 15: A model of school development
Adapted from Carter (2015)

Crucially, his model makes it self-evident that the leadership approach needed at each stage will need to vary to suit the context. This theme will be explored in more detail in Section D of the book, particularly in Topic 37 on leadership styles.

Key points

- Do you or colleagues use anonymous survey data from pupils, parents and staff to regularly assess the culture and climate of your school?
- How do you monitor the work of your staff and their performance? Are the systems you have established at a whole-school level being robustly and transparently implemented?
- Do your staff understand why observation and monitoring is important and have they bought in to the concept?
- What are senior leaders doing to moderate and validate the judgements that are being made?

Topic 10

Monitoring and data

It is a capital mistake to theorise
before one has data.
Arthur Conan Doyle

Monitoring within a team, school or organisation enables you, at any point in time, to know where things are. It's how you really do know the deal that your pupils are getting. It is a way of properly understanding your culture.

There are a number of approaches to monitoring that you can implement and the more you link them together, the more accurate your monitoring will be.

Learning walks give you an idea of where every class and teacher is in terms of teaching and learning and the learning environment itself. These walks tend to fall on a spectrum: they can be extremely formal, for example ten-minute observations with written feedback; focused, such as a weekly or daily focus on marking, differentiation, or assessment for learning; or a 'pop in' which would involve an interaction with the teacher, interaction with some or most of the pupils and gauging the quality of teaching and learning. No doubt your school or organisation will have developed a set of working practices.

However it is practically organised, there are some key fundamentals about monitoring to remember:

- Everyone involved needs to accept the approach and buy in to the idea of how it is being done.
- You need to ensure that everyone knows exactly why monitoring is so important and that the outcome will contribute to the raising of standards.
- There should be guidelines for the way in which learning walks will be done. What can people expect in the form of feedback, how often will it be and what will they be expected to do with it?

You and your colleagues need to stick to these points so that you deliver a consistent, fair and helpful monitoring process.

Work scrutinies are the same; marking and planning should be reviewed regularly. Again, clear expectations that are well communicated help everyone and ensure good buy-in. You might want to create a calendar of scrutinies at the start of the year and an organised pro-forma of what to expect in terms of when and what the feedback will be, to help embed open, transparent and systematic self-evaluation. In addition, why not build up an abundance of excellent practice which is modelled and shared to help everyone know where the bar has been set and to celebrate good practice? If the climate of learning walks is one of recognition and reward rather than fear and blame, underpinned with a set of basic expectations, their power to support teacher development is significant.

A key consideration with all monitoring is how you get the balance right between assuring yourself things are as they should be and not making colleagues feel like you don't trust them. In the end, this comes down to your own professional judgement, based on reliable information on both performance and morale.

Using data

It's a bit of a cliché but as the old adage suggests, continually weighing a pig doesn't make it any fatter. That's the point made by critics who think that some schools spend too much time and energy measuring anything that moves at the expense of concentrating on ensuring lessons are well-planned, well-executed and fun for pupils. Indeed, there are schools that spend a lot of time collecting all kinds of data that has negligible impact on pupils' learning outcomes. Tables and tables of information sitting on a marvellous database do little in themselves to drive up standards.

But farmers would argue otherwise. There will always be a need to weigh a pig from to time to time to make sure there is nothing wrong with it. It ought to be gaining weight at a certain rate – if it isn't, then why not? Monitoring the pig's weight allows the farmer to intervene if there is a problem. It allows the farmer to reflect on what works best and what doesn't seem to be working. It allows the farmer to try out new ideas and evaluate whether they are a success.

In other words, when it comes to data, you need to model yourself on the farming profession! You need to know how well pupils are progressing; your team need to have data that will help them reflect on what is working and what is not. They need to be able to intervene when an individual or a particular group of pupils appears to be falling behind. They also need to be able to see the overall 'big picture'. Are there changes that need to be made to the curriculum or to a particular scheme of learning?

What is important here is the frequency and accuracy of data and the pupil-by-pupil analysis that leads to timely and focused planning. This can only happen if data is current and has been collected efficiently and accurately. Basing intervention on out-of-date data is a waste of everyone's time and will fail to secure buy-in from staff or pupils. Hopefully your whole-school systems will have all this in place. If colleagues are telling you otherwise, maybe it is time to look again at how you organise your data processes.

Whatever the practicalities of the process, accuracy is critical. This means it is essential that you have robust systems for moderating pupils' achievements, both through work scrutiny and high quality testing. For middle leaders in particular, regularly allocating time to this in meetings – where this is possible – is a useful way of making sure everyone is working to the same set of expectations about what constitutes a particular grade or level. Some teams find it helpful to keep portfolios of work as part of the evidence that can support this approach.

I would offer one caveat here. Learning doesn't always happen in a linear way. All of us working in schools need to use our professional judgement to get the balance right between understanding precisely what pupils can and can't do, and trying to define a broad level that they have reached. Some of the recent changes to assessments in England have been introduced with this in mind. Putting aside the way in which these changes have been introduced, the idea of 'best-fit' assessment when it comes to making formative judgements was a feature of previous assessment systems that wasn't really in pupils' interests.

As well as thinking about individual pupil progress and interventions, looking at the data from a curriculum point of view, by using question-level analysis (QLA), for example, is another powerful tool to raise standards. In any given area, is there a skill/content area in which pupils under-perform in a particular class or in all classes? Is there a subject knowledge gap within teaching that needs to be addressed? Do boys perform better or worse than girls in a particular area?

The data should be used for effective conversations and comparisons around these types of questions within teams. All staff should feel a clear sense of accountability for the pupils in their care and be clear about their role in providing accurate and timely data and planning effective interventions. There should be a healthy balance between challenge and support for both pupils and staff. Linked to this, as mentioned already, it is important to ensure you build in formal opportunities to celebrate success and recognise achievements. Again, this applies equally to staff and pupils.

Key points

- Do you have a good balance and breadth of monitoring approaches?
- Do you use the data you collect about pupil progress in a way that supports their learning?
- How do you know the data you collect is accurate?
- Would there be any benefit in doing this more collaboratively?

- How much do you rely on interventions to retrospectively repair gaps in knowledge or skills?
- Do you use QLA to review and re-plan your curriculum or schemes of learning?
- Would there be any benefit in doing this more collaboratively?

Topic 11

Performance and predispositions

My bad habits aren't my title. My strengths and my talent are my title.
Layne Staley

Many of the suggestions in earlier topics about how you can get to know yourself apply equally when thinking about others. Just like you, they will have their own predispositions, strengths and areas for growth. But do you know what these are? Do you consciously and deliberately think about your approach with individuals you interact with and reflect those differences? Or do you just tend to work with everyone the same way, perhaps more reflecting your own preferences than what is going to get the best out of them?

Using personality tools and 360 surveys can be helpful. So too, can using data effectively to monitor outcomes and performance, as we saw in Topic 10.

There is also huge potential to understand colleagues from your day-to-day interactions with them, whether you are a middle leader, senior leader or running a school or group of schools. Whatever your circumstances, there will be key people with whom you work that it will be useful for you to know and understand well, including those that report to you, your peers and others who may be more senior than you (including governors and trustees). So how do you make the most of these interactions?

At its heart, your approach needs to focus on taking the time and effort to listen to and observe colleagues carefully. While the assertion from Mehrabian (1972) that only 7% of communication comes from what is said; whereas 38% is through tone of voice and 55% from reading body language, is often taken out of its original context, it is a helpful reminder that we need to be attuned to all three of these aspects of communication. It can also be useful to develop a habit that Topic 38 of this book will develop in much more detail: that of asking first. By asking neutral questions, you can establish much more quickly where someone is with their thinking or level of motivation on an issue.

What are you looking for?

In simple terms, leaders need to try to understand others' competence, preferred ways of working and their motivations. If you are able to work these out, you are in a position to tailor your approach accordingly. Let's say you are introducing a new idea. Some of your colleagues may be keen to properly understand how it fits into the wider strategy before getting into the detail. Others, on the other hand, need to understand the detail of how something is going to work in practice before they are interested in its place within the wider strategy. If you were to pitch a new idea to an individual and didn't factor these preferences into your explanation, you would inevitably create reduced buy-in or engagement for the project from those individuals.

Similarly, some of your team will be much happier if you have a clear implementation plan already mapped out so they can see the way ahead is organised and decided. For others, this matters much less, in fact some colleagues may prefer not to have too much tied down too soon, as this may limit your flexibility to amend your approach as you go. LM Persona – available on the Leadership Matters website – is an easy way to develop this wider understanding of your colleagues.

Playing to strengths

One other key reason for getting to know your team well is to find out what they are good at and make sure you and colleagues take the opportunity to play to their strengths. In her great article 'In praise of the incomplete leader', Deborah Ancona (2007) argues that the very best leaders know what it is they are good at and find other people to lead on the areas they are not. Apart from this making sense at the most basic level, it is also an approach that builds individuals' levels of motivation for two reasons: firstly, because you or a colleague has identified their strength in the first place; and secondly, because we all like doing things we are good at. So from every perspective, make sure you not only have the right people on the bus, but also that they are sitting in the right seats.

In their book *Leadership: all you need to know*, Pendleton and Furnham (2012) have taken this idea and created a simple but effective model for thinking about how to take into account both the performance of colleagues and their natural predispositions. Figure 16 shows this.

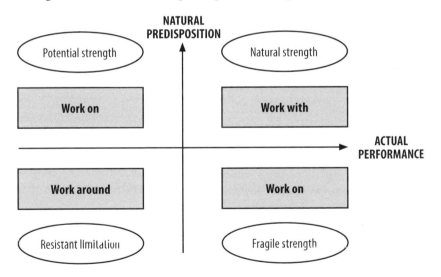

Figure 16: Playing to strengths
Adapted from Pendleton and Furnham (2012)

For areas where an individual has *natural strengths*, it's important to give them the chance to excel and continue developing, with the aim of becoming even better and the go-to person within your team or organisation for that particular area.

Potential strengths are those areas which, with just a little attention, a colleague could be great at. This is generally because they have a predisposition towards it and just need to give it some focus.

Fragile strengths are things that an individual can do well if they put their mind to it, but success in these areas doesn't come easily. For example, all school leaders need to be able to use data effectively. For some, this will be a natural strength. For others, it takes practice and focus. But it is achievable.

In contrast, what the model calls *resistant limitations* are those things an individual isn't good at and frankly has no interest or motivation to try to improve at. I have heard this described as the things that were in your Year 8 report that still seem to come up in your annual appraisal now! Pendleton and Furnham argue that rather than to continue year after year to make this a focus for development, one is much better trying to find a workaround, which usually involves finding someone else to do it.

The more senior one is, the easier it is to play to one's own strengths and delegate tasks that play to colleagues' strengths, as Ancona argues one should. I must sound a note of caution, however. There are some things one simply cannot delegate to others. For a classroom teacher, for example, one cannot and should not delegate the task of managing relationships and behaviour to someone else. In the end, there has to be a decent fit between an individual and their role. If this is missing, then it's not good news for the individual or the pupils.

Key points

- How well do you know your team?
- Do you support colleagues to play to their strengths?
- Do you enable team members to work on the right areas?
- Are you open to helping to find workarounds where they seem appropriate?

Topic 12

Performance, behaviours and values

It is not easy in this world for one person to understand the next one.
Goethe

Managing differential performance in others

As well as knowing about how others prefer to work and playing to their strengths, the very best leaders in schools, at all levels, are good at knowing how well colleagues in their team are performing and respond accordingly. Pendleton and Furnham (2012) have developed an interesting model (Figure 17) which suggests leaders can group colleagues according to the behaviours and values of others and their performance at work.

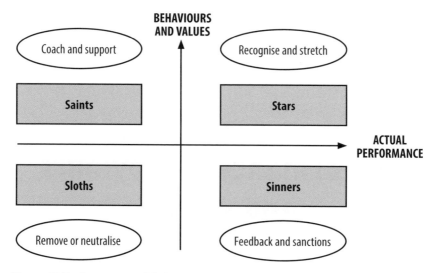

Figure 17: Performance and behaviours
Adapted from Pendleton and Furnham (2012)

Let's begin with the stars. These are your high performers who are doing a great job and work in a way that is absolutely in line with the culture and climate you wish to create. They are also the group you need to be careful not to overlook or take for granted. Just like you, they need to be challenged, stretched and recognised for what they do. The more they feel they have a say in their future, the better, but you need to make sure you don't over promise. They will usually appreciate development opportunities, whether formal or informal. They may also be useful when it comes to coaching others, in particular your saints.

At the other extreme are your sloths. These are individuals who are performing poorly and are potentially having a pernicious effect on your culture and climate. You need to quickly understand what sits behind their poor outcomes and attitude and give them very clear and unambiguous feedback about what needs to change in relation to both. Make it clear they are making choices about their future. They then need to improve very quickly or there will be consequences. Ultimately, and with dignity, you need to be prepared to work out a way for them to leave fast.

Your saints are very well-meaning members of your team, but they are just not very good. As with the sloths, you need to take time to understand what is stopping them from doing a good job and then make sure they are supported and coached to improve. So long as they continue to improve at a sufficient rate, you should continue to support them. Only if they seem to have peaked at a point that is below your expectations, should you consider how they might also move on to pastures new.

Finally, the toughest group of all are your sinners! These are high performing individuals who get great results and achieve strongly. But they do it in a way that undermines the culture and climate you are trying to establish. They don't, for example, get reports written on time nor follow behaviour systems properly. They are often disloyal about your leadership and others in the wider team. In short, they are an annoying thorn in your side. If you have inherited a team whose performance across the board is poor, you may decide you have to live with your sinner(s) for a while – just having anyone who is performing is the priority. But if, over time, it feels like you have reached a tipping point where their negative effect on the wider team is exceeding the positive impact of their own performance, action to address their shortcomings is probably needed. Unlike the saints, who need coaching, what they need is to be given very clear feedback about what needs to change and by when. Coaching probably isn't what's needed. They just need to decide to change or to face the consequences. Ultimately, they may need to leave too, if changes don't occur.

Most schools are better at dealing with saints than sinners, partly as there is usually much more written down about the levels of competence that need to be achieved. But having clear statements of expectations around behaviours expected are equally important if one is tackle what, for sinners, are more likely to be disciplinary issues than those relating to competence.

I don't think Pendleton and Furnham are suggesting you should put each of your staff into one of the boxes and label them in this rather 'black and white' way, people are usually more complex than this. But the model does provide a useful way for you to think about how different individuals may need different approaches that are centred on them rather than a general response to any given situation, regardless of context.

The final part of this topic gives some practical strategies that might be useful when thinking about your team. These are suggestions, again from Pendleton and Furnham, are about what might be worth considering in each area.

Stars
- Biggest challenge is keeping them motivated, engaged, progressing
- Make sure they know they are recognised and valued
- Careful, selective feedback
- Involve them in setting their own goals to a greater extent
- Understand their career goals and commit to supporting them
- Delegate more responsibility – enlarge their role, special projects
- Give them exposure to more senior colleagues
- Offer the opportunity to represent the group or team
- Coaching and developing others in the team, such as the saints
- Clear, unambiguous expectations about career progression – don't promise what you can't deliver

Saints
- Find out what the cause of the underperformance is
- They may not understand expectations or goals
- Don't have skills or haven't learned them yet
- Lack of motivation
- Don't realise they are not 'delivering' – no feedback
- Wrong fit for job
- Something in private life
- Give feedback – specific, examples relevant, timely
- Coaching, training, development
- Support and buddying, for example from a star
- Re-define job responsibilities

- Set short term goals and give frequent feedback
- Get them to take ownership
- Keep track of actions and performance discussions

Sinners

- Find out the underlying cause (arrogance, boredom, don't care)
- Confront the behaviour *assertively*, explain the impact on others, hold the mirror up
- Beware of the impact of tolerating poor behaviour and values on the rest of team and colleagues
- Get them to 'own' their behaviour and the impact on others
- Explain that behaviour and values is part of how their performance is judged, not just their results
- A few clear rules and boundaries
- Make sure they commit to specific changes
- Make sure they own the action plan
- Connect the behaviour or attitude with something they care about
- Peer pressure
- Consequences for not changing – get them to accept it is in their hands – it's their choice
- Keep track of actions and performance discussions
- Be prepared to move them on if you judge the negative impact on the team or organisation outweighs the positive

Sloths

- Act fast – quick diagnosis of underlying causes – as per saints and sinners – decide if it is primarily a skill, motivation or attitude problem – employ the same tactics as for saints or sinners
- Feedback, feedback, feedback
- Clear communications of expectation of improvement, if not, consequences

- Get them to own the plan
- Be clear about how long you will give them to turn around
- Keep track of actions and performance discussions
- Be prepared to fire them if they don't improve fast

Key points

- Do you understand others' personality predispositions? Do you use any personality tools to support this?
- Do you use 360 reviews or other mechanisms to better understand the performance of others around you?
- How good are you at really focusing on what others are saying or what their tone of voice and body language is telling you?
- How well do you deliberately play to others' strengths?
- How good are you at consciously differentiating the way you work with colleagues who display different behaviours or levels of performance?

Section C

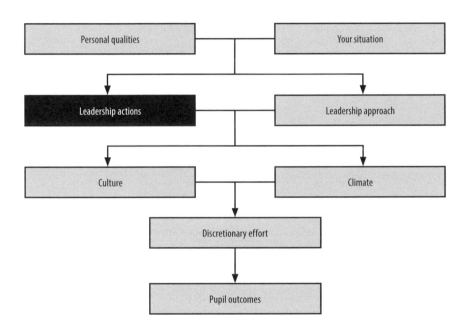

Leadership actions

Leadership is an action, not a position
Donald McGannon

This is the largest section of the book and looks at each element of David Pendleton's (2012) Primary Colours model in turn:

- Set the strategic direction
- Create alignment
- Build and sustain relationships
- Create teams
- Deliver results and get things done
- Plan and organise

There are four topics for each element of the model, each containing useful theory as well as lots of practical advice and ideas.

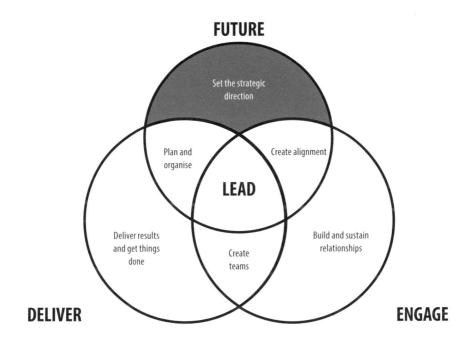

FUTURE

Set the strategic direction

Plan and organise

Create alignment

LEAD

Deliver results and get things done

Create teams

Build and sustain relationships

DELIVER

ENGAGE

Set the strategic direction

What's the use of running if you are not on the right road?
German proverb

This section is the first of six in which we look at each of the leadership elements contained within David Pendleton's Primary Colours model (2012).

Setting the strategic direction for your team or organisation is a fundamental prerequisite for leadership success. Without the clarity of where you want to go and how you are going to get there, pupil outcomes just won't be as good. With this in mind, Topic 13 examines the concepts of vision, values and strategy. In Topic 14, we explore the findings of the highly respected meta-analysis carried out by Viviane Robinson and her team (2011) which looks at what it is that leaders do that has the biggest impact on pupil outcomes. Topic 15 builds on the influential work of Carol Dweck (2012) to consider ways to build self-belief, resilience and motivation in pupils. Finally, in Topic 16, we draw on the work of Daniel Kahneman (2011) to explore how we tend to make decisions and how we can all develop better decision-making habits.

Topic 13

Vision, values and strategy

The best CEOs I know are teachers, and at the core of what they teach is strategy.
Michael Porter

When we heard from heads of schools that had been judged outstanding three or four times at the G2G conferences I ran, a striking feature that regularly emerged was the importance of clarity of vision, values and strategy. The heads talked about the importance of a clear vision and shared a common purpose as well as, equally importantly, having clarity around the detail of how systems and procedures work in schools: the strategy for achieving them. Topic 17 will focus on the latter, exploring the importance of a clearly understood and agreed clarity on the 'way we do things around here'.

This topic will focus on the importance of vision, values and strategy, drawing upon themes from the schools' presentations at G2G conferences, in addition to some of the points made in Jim Collins' *Good to Great* in considering what he describes as his *hedgehog concept* as well as examining some of the evidence from Peter Matthews' 2009 Ofsted publication.

We shall also consider the important role that good governance plays in supporting the development of the right strategic approach, drawing on the excellent publication, *A Framework for Governance*, published by the National Governors' Association in 2015.

It is common sense that successful schools will have clear goals. They need know what they are for and what they want to achieve. This may be expressed in very simple terms such as ensuring that a school does its utmost to help every young person achieve as much as he or she can. But in the very best schools there is also a vision for the special ingredients in the circumstances of that particular school that go towards making it a success in that context.

One very powerful way of thinking about this has been suggested by Simon Sinek in his best-selling book: *Start with why* (2011).

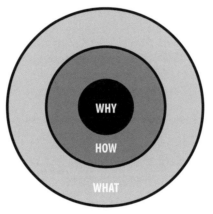

Figure 18: Start with why
Simon Sinek (2011)

Sinek argues that most organisations can describe *what* they do, some can articulate *how* they do what they do and very few know *why* they do what they do. He believes the best organisations turn this on its head and start from the inside out, by thinking about the *why* first. For us in the schools' sector, we have a huge advantage in this respect. The reasons we come to work and the reasons schools exist are well understood and important for all of us in the profession. But taking time to consider properly the way in which we seek to achieve success is where the importance of the *how*, the strategy, emerges. One can then use this to work out the detail of the *what*.

At Leadership Matters we have used this approach to think about our own work. Here is our thinking to date as an example of how the model works:

WHY: *Because leadership matters*

- We believe leadership isn't a rank: it exists at every level and we know it makes a real difference to outcomes for pupils
- We should never stop seeking to enhance the culture and climate in our schools
- We have a responsibility to inspire and support the next generation of school leaders

HOW: *By empowering schools to create their own leadership learning and development*

- By provoking a quality dialogue around leadership learning and development
- By creating a shared language for effective leadership behaviours
- By being 'with you, for you' as a profession

WHAT: *An international leadership community for education professionals*

- Supported by trusted diagnostic tools, high quality learning resources and inspirational membership events
- Created for individuals, teams, schools and groups of schools
- Designed to be user-friendly, flexible and exceptional value

So how do schools go about arriving at their own vision, values and strategy? From an individual perspective, experiences both as a child and as an adult will have shaped the view of what an ideal school should look like, how it should feel and, importantly, how it might work. Almost unconsciously, school leaders and governors know what they want to achieve. However, translating these aspirations into a form of words can be far from easy.

There is also the question of how much the vision of a school should only reflect the views of the head, leadership team or the governing body. There is no doubt that the more people are involved in the process of defining a school's vision, including pupils themselves, their parents, other school leaders and the staff, the greater the sense of ownership and buy-in.

A shared sense of direction is vital in any school's success. However, consultation of this kind comes with a strong health warning and needs skilful handling by school leaders. The last thing one wants to end up with is a series of bland statements that could apply to any school, which everyone agrees with, but which don't really end up saying anything distinctive.

This challenge is magnified in the context of a group of schools. If you are system leader, you will no doubt recognise the tension between allowing each school its own identity and ensuring that your group of schools can define its distinctive qualities. One way to square this circle, which draws on the giraffe concept I mentioned in Topic 1, is for a group of schools to define together its key principles (the long neck issues) and then allow each school to interpret and refine these in their own particular context (the markings).

Jim Collins is clear about the importance of organisations really narrowing down the focus of what they are trying to achieve and specifically how they will go about achieving it. To keep the animal analogies going for a moment, he calls this his *hedgehog concept* based upon the parable of the hedgehog and the fox. Every day the fox tries to outwit the hedgehog, trying a range of different strategies to beat him. What does the hedgehog do? The same thing every time: roll up into a prickly ball with success guaranteed every time. The school that jumps on the bandwagon every time a new initiative comes out or the head gets a bright idea is the school that may be good but is unlikely to be consistently outstanding.

Devising strategy

In its excellent publication, *A Framework for Governance* (2015) the National Governors' Association identifies three key objectives for any governing board, whether they have oversight as governors of a single school or as trustees with responsibility of a group of schools:

- Setting the strategic direction
- Holding the headteacher to account for the educational performance of the school
- Ensuring financial health, probity and value for money

The first of these squarely puts strategy at the heart of governance. The role of governors or trustees is to ensure a school has a long-term strategy based on a clear shared vision. Making sure there is also clarity on where the boundary between strategic input and operational delivery sits is also critical. The following diagram summarises how this should work in practice.

School strategy

Agreed by governing board. Setting out the vision for the school and its broad ambitions.

Developed in discussion with leaders, teachers, parents and learners.

School development plan

Developed by senior leaders based on the strategic plan.

With details of how the strategy will be turned into reality.

Agreed by governing board.

Implementation in practice

Done by senior leaders and staff.

Monitored by governors, parents and learners.

Figure 19: Setting the strategy – the role of governance
Adapted from A Framework for Governance
National Governors' Association (2015)

The NGA recommend the vision should:

- be ambitious but achievable
- take into account the school's current context
- take account of stakeholders' views
- be agreed and owned by the board.

To support the ability of a governing board to play this strategic role, the members require a number of key competencies:

- They understand their role and how it complements that of the headteacher.
- They have a range of skills that brings something extra to the school and can develop a strategic vision.

- They have technical knowledge – of education, data, statutory responsibilities and performance management in particular.
- They want to see and hear from middle and senior leaders about their work – and challenge them on it.
- They have the skills and time to be a visible presence in the school.
- They set challenging targets for performance at all levels, including in achievement, teaching and senior management work.
- They can form their own analysis of the school's performance without relying on the headteacher.

Monitoring delivery

A great strategy without great delivery is a waste of time. As Winston Churchill reminds us: 'However beautiful the strategy, one should occasionally look at the results'. School leaders and governors need to have robust systems in place to ensure a strategy is being implemented and know the impact on outcomes for pupils. Ensuring objectives are SMART (specific, measurable, achievable, relevant and time-bound) is important. Developing a set of key performance indicators (KPIs) allows this monitoring to focus on the key elements of the strategy. This needs to happen as part of a regular cycle of review. There also needs to be robust triangulation and verification of the data and information that comes to both senior leaders and governors. Too often where a school is failing, the picture painted is that all seems fine and then it turns out it wasn't. Governors need to be confident that the picture being painted for them is a real one. Critically, this is about governors and trustees really knowing their schools and, as a result, being able to ask great questions that challenge and properly hold to account, as well as recognise and celebrate success.

Objective – strategy – tactics

In his 2015 book *Winners* Alastair Campbell, the former director of communications for Tony Blair, talks about the importance of using OST: objective – strategy – tactics. His main point is that once you have an objective, it is important to consider what your main *single* strategy is for achieving it. He reflects back on the 1997 UK general election. Their objective: for Labour to win the election. The strategy: we are New Labour. The tactics: a whole series of actions and policies that fitted the overall strategy, such as the removal of Clause IV, making friends with the right-wing press (Rupert Murdoch, in particular) and a new party logo. Outcome: they won the election. Contrast this with Labour's approach to the election in 2010 and you can see how there wasn't really an overall game plan. Yes, the objective was clear: regain power. But the tactics didn't add up to a coherent strategy. In fact, some of the policies and messaging seemed contradictory. For example, the party was at pains to point out that Labour 'is a friend of business' and 'the economy is safe with us'. Yet at the same time, they were advocating a cap on both energy prices and rents in private sector housing. Of course, hindsight is a wonderful thing, but whatever one's political standpoint, the analysis does resonate. Figure 20 takes the OST approach and applies it in a secondary school context.

Objectives (ideally just 2 or 3 in any given year; maximum of 6; need to be SMART)
• Increase the number of pupils getting to university to 160 by 2022
Strategy (only one for each objective)
• Building independence and a growth mindset
Tactics (linked to each strategy – keep as simple as possible)
• Praise effort and process • Stop using extrinsic rewards such as Vivo points • Organise university trips in Years 7, 9 and 12 • Bring successful former pupils back in Years 8, 10, 11 and 13 to inspire pupils • Develop extended project approach from Year 7, embedded x-curricular • Provide wide co-curricular opportunities, including sports, arts, travel, adventure, debating, volunteering, camps • Organise inspirational visiting speakers who grew up locally

Figure 20: Using OST
Adapted from Alastair Campbell in *Winners* (2015)

The critical point here is that, for any given objective, you should ideally aim for only one overall strategy and then line up your tactics underneath this.

In my view, the most successful schools are those that work out a successful strategy and stick to it, making sure that it is followed day in day out. Having a clarity around a core purpose is essential, however simply expressed and however it is arrived at. Even the few words that make up the average school's motto can speak volumes, providing something around which all those who are connected with the school can unite.

As an example, one school I have worked with recently has developed very clear and simple guidelines for all aspects of the school day. There are three key statements that underpin all that the school does and can be applied to any situation by staff or pupils: 'the street stops at the gate', 'a relentless focus on high standards' and 'there are no barriers or excuses to great learning or achievement'.

Without this clear sense of where a school is meant to be going, there is a strong likelihood that it simply goes nowhere. Staff, pupils and parents cannot operate with hundreds of policies circulating around their brains. They need clarity around a series of key principles that underpin the way things are expected to happen, and when they are not sure about something they can refer back to their understanding of these principles and apply them appropriately. The chances are they will be following policy, so long as the policy itself is consistent with the school's core values and agreed ways of working.

The same applies to school leadership at all levels. When decisions need to be made by leaders in a school there is nothing more helpful than clear guidance, a clear steer, about how they should be made. It is this clarity that breeds trust and confidence from everyone within a school community. It is also what gives senior and middle leaders the platform upon which to make decisions within their own sphere of influence, knowing they will be in line with the overall strategic approach but nuanced by their own circumstances. In other words, once again, the *giraffe concept* in action.

The importance of keeping focused

The final point to make about clarity of vision and strategy is around the benefits that can come from having a clear view about what a school focuses on and therefore, by definition, what it decides not to do. As Stephen Covey suggests, 'The main thing is to keep the main thing the main thing'!

A clear message from many of the successful schools I have worked with has been that they are very good at distinguishing between those things that help them achieve their core purpose and those that may run the risk of diluting their intent. We all know the temptation to engage with every initiative, particularly when inspection frameworks and other national expectations may encourage schools to do so.

Those schools that have a well-developed set of goals are well placed to make decisions about these possible areas of development. But the very best schools will not only have clarity around their goals but will also have developed a clear understanding throughout the institution of how those goals are achieved. It is by measuring against these ways of working that judgements can be made about whether a particular initiative would be worthwhile.

As Peter Matthews puts it, 'Characteristically, these schools are able to maintain a sharp focus, rigour and consistency in the basics, while innovating and developing their provision further to bring new gains in pupils' learning and achievement. They do not overstretch themselves and are careful not to jump on bandwagons. Middle and senior leaders have a thorough understanding of which developments are right for their school and which are not. They scrutinise new ideas and developments and ask hard questions about what value they will have for pupils' learning and achievement.

Crucially, these leaders also understand how much capacity the school has to support innovation and development (and they actively work to strengthen it). While the schools are not afraid to take risks, the risks that they do take are careful, calculated and considered. Anything that is done is carefully planned and meticulously implemented.'

In other words, the absolute focus on the core business of the school is maintained. Innovation, creativity and risk taking are encouraged, but only when they help deliver clearly identified goals for the school.

One academy group in England has taken the idea of clarity and applied it brilliantly to the way they define their approach to leadership. Figure 21 summarises how the ARK group of schools views the three critical elements that make for highly effective school leadership.

Brutally consistent in designing clear policies, communicating them simply, and implementing them to the highest standard.	Respectfully relentless in developing people and helping put them in a position to maximise impact.	Rigorously joyful in embracing the opportunities and challenges of educating young people, having fun, and celebrating success.

Figure 21: The ARK approach to school leadership
Adapted from Sims (2017)

It's interesting to note how this approach resonates with what Steve Radcliffe in his FED model suggests matters most in leadership more generally.

Key points

- Are you clear about exactly what you are trying to achieve and the two or three key elements of your work that will enable you to achieve it?
- Are governors or trustees at the heart of the development of your strategic approach and the monitoring of its implementation and impact?
- Is the concept of OST (objective – strategy – tactics) something that might be useful for you to adopt in your context?
- Are you good at rejecting initiatives that may distract you from your focus?
- Are you clear about your core principles and do you set the highest expectations in all aspects of your work?
- Do leaders at all levels take decisions based on internal and external research and evidence?
- Are you aware of the most common causes of decision-making bias? Could the STOP model (Topic 16) be a useful way to help you make good decisions?

Topic 14

Leading for maximum impact

> But seriously, I think overall in the scheme of things winning an Emmy is not important. Let's get our priorities straight. I think we all know what's really important in life – winning an Oscar.
>
> Ellen DeGeneres

Much has been written recently about teaching becoming a more evidence-based profession. Without evidence, we have no empirical proof that strategies and interventions work, we only have individual opinion and judgement. For too long, our judgements about which reading strategies work or which class size is most effective have been based on incorrect assumptions developed by teachers and leaders from just their personal experience without considering other evidence.

As Dr Gary Jones suggests in *Evidence based principles* (2016), an evidence-based approach is about combining one's own experience, observation and analysis with what other external evidence suggests. That way you can attempt to work out what is going to work for your pupils in your context. It is also about making sure you don't adopt any externally generated idea without first checking its credentials. For example, we can look at two ideas that have swept education over the past decade: visual, audio and kinaesthetic (VAK) learning styles and Brain Gym. Both were thought to tap into the way pupils learn to help them improve cognition and outcomes. Both were taken on by thousands of schools as an answer to pupil engagement and learning, but subsequent research has suggested there is little basis for these ideas (Coffield *et al*, 2004).

As teachers and leaders, we often base our strategies and interventions on personal experience, or what we have seen work. This is why middle leaders can sometimes feel that more senior members of staff who have seen more and have more experience, believe they know more or can tell them why something will not work. In reality though, it is hard to know without also looking at the evidence. Good strategies might be considered not to work because the teacher implemented them poorly. Evidence gives you the proof and grounding to have confidence in your strategy, an empirical basis to disprove the doubters and a means to get the whole team to focus on what works.

Accessing evidence is becoming easier. The two most useful sources of evidence are John Hattie's *Visible Learning* (2009) and the Education Endowment Foundation's (EEF) *Toolkit*. Both are connected and give effect sizes (a measure of how effective an intervention is) for a range of pupil interventions such as class size, homework, and assessment for learning. The EEF toolkit also gives relative cost and value for money data so you can judge which interventions to use. The Education Endowment Foundation disseminates the results from the evaluations it has run.

Leadership effectiveness

Time is a precious commodity for anyone working in schools. So, for school leaders in particular, making sure you spend your time on things that make the biggest difference is crucial. In Topic 33, we examine generic ways of prioritising what you do, but this topic looks at one piece of research in particular.

When it comes to what the evidence tells us on what it is that leaders do that appears to make the biggest difference to pupil outcomes at a strategic level, in my view there is nothing better than the 2011 meta-analysis that Viviane Robinson and her colleagues from the University of Auckland conducted.

As with any meta-analysis, one needs to exercise a little professional scepticism. There are those among the educational research community who would suggest that Viviane Robinson has overstated her findings. But as a school leader with over 25 years' experience, the findings of the Auckland team certainly resonate with me.

Figure 22 summarises their work and identifies the five key activities that leaders undertake that appear make the biggest difference to pupil outcomes.

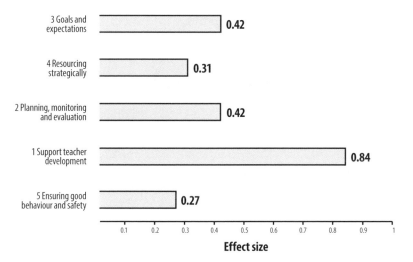

Figure 22: What leaders do that has the biggest impact on pupil outcomes
Adapted from Viviane Robinson's *Pupil-centred leadership* (2011)

All of the themes identified in the outcomes in Figure 22 resonate with much that is covered in this book. But it is striking how the impact of one factor, supporting teacher development, is so much more impactful than its next nearest statistical neighbour. It only goes to show how important it is for leaders at all levels to create the time to quite simply focus on helping teachers be better teachers.

The zone of growth

The last model I would like to share in this topic originates from the work of Yerkes and Dodson (1908). The model suggests that there is a powerful link between how challenging tasks are to complete and the impact they have on our cognitive development. If we stay in our comfort zone, doing things we find easy most of the time, unsurprisingly our personal development is steady but pretty low. When we are in the zone of stretch or growth, the impact on our learning and development is suddenly much higher.

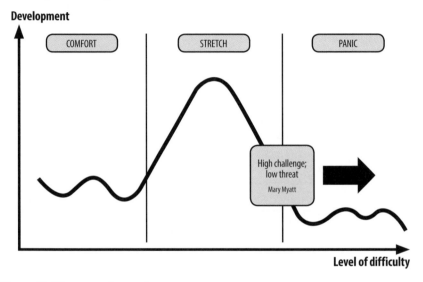

Figure 23: The zone of growth
Adapted from Yerkes and Dodson (1908)

Typically, the model suggests the zone of growth is 10–15% outside one's zone of comfort, although I am not sure how one is meant to actually measure this! But the broad concept is powerful and can be applied to teachers and leaders. Pupils should be in the zone of stretch for large parts of their day or we are doing them a disservice. Leaders should be creating the culture and climate that creates high levels of discretionary effort (see Topic 2) among staff, so they are motivated to be a little better tomorrow than they were yesterday. Of course, in all cases, what actually constitutes the zone of stretch will vary from pupil to pupil and between colleagues.

There is however, a limit to how far we can push the level of challenge. If the level of difficulty is too high, and I would argue this can be in terms of cognitive challenge or through the sheer volume of work that is expected, then personal well-being and self-belief start to become an issue and individuals will find themselves in the zone of panic or stress. If individual pupils or staff are in this zone for long periods of time, there is a risk of mental health issues developing.

Having read Mary Myatt's inspiring book, *High Challenge, Low Threat* (2016), I am reminded of our ability as both teachers and leaders to metaphorically move where the line separating growth and panic actually sits. If we can create an environment of mutual trust and respect, where it is OK to try hard things even if we make mistakes, then we can enable pupils and colleagues to take on more challenging tasks without feeling stressed or panicked.

So, if supporting teacher development should be a key strategic objective for school leaders, how exactly should you go about it in a way that maximises activity in the zone of growth? Topic 30 explores in detail how incremental coaching can support this goal, while Topics 39 and 40 explore the benefits of a coaching approach to leadership more generally.

Key points

- How much time to you and your colleagues devote to directly or indirectly supporting teacher learning and development?
- How useful is the concept of the zones of comfort, growth and panic?
- How do you help teachers to be better teachers in practice? Might incremental coaching be a useful approach to take?

Topic 15

Pupil self-belief and motivation

Some people say I have attitude. Maybe
I do, but I think you have to. You have to
believe in yourself when no one else does
– that makes you a winner right there.
Venus Williams

When it comes to strategy, context is everything. What will work in one context may not quite work in the same way in another. For many schools however, one common challenge is quite often related to pupils' self-belief and motivation. You can have the very best teachers, and a fabulous curriculum being brilliantly taught in classrooms where behaviour is good, but pupils may not be achieving as well as they might. The analogy of the horse and water comes to mind.

In my work leading the London Challenge *Good to Great* programme, one of the most striking features of great schools has been the way they have been able to create a culture of aspiration and achievement for their pupils. By creating self-motivated and self-disciplined young people who share the vision and take ownership of their own learning, the best schools have been able to co-create success for the whole school community.

This topic aims to summarise some of the key things successful schools do to enable pupils to become independent and self-motivated learners, as set out in Figure 24.

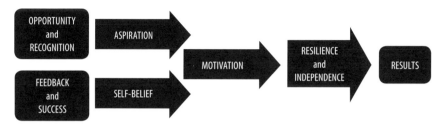

Figure 24: Building self-belief and motivation

A key role for schools in helping pupils have aspirations is showing them what is 'out there'. Exposing pupils to broader horizons through great visits and great visitors can form a crucial element in this approach. What can make this even more powerful is if pupils recognise people who look and sound like them doing amazing things with their lives. Suddenly pupils, especially those from more challenging contexts, are thinking 'OK, people like me do jobs like that' rather than thinking they are jobs done by other people.

But having an aspiration on its own isn't enough. Pupils need to believe in themselves and what they can achieve. As Muijs and Reynolds (2011) point out, 'The effect of achievement on self-concept is stronger than the effect of self-concept on achievement'. It seems to me that this means that all the adults that work with pupils need to develop habits in two important areas.

Firstly, they need to ensure pupils experience genuine success. That doesn't mean they aren't challenged and only do easy things. Quite the reverse. It means pupils engage with challenging knowledge and skills and as a result, demonstrate great learning and ultimately great results. Equally important is that they are then in a position to develop self-belief and confidence.

Secondly, as Carol Dweck would argue, pupils need to be given the right kind of feedback that helps them build on their successes as well as praising them not for their intelligence but for the effort and the process of learning that they have undertaken. There isn't the space in this publication to say much more about the concept of growth mindset, and it is fair to say that the evidence to date about the effectiveness of this approach is still being gathered and peer-reviewed. There are however, some excellent books which focus on this, not least Chris Hildrew's *Becoming a growth mindset school* (2018).

To summarise, if we can create a situation where pupils want to achieve something and believe they can, then this combination is potentially very powerful. This drive is then the trigger for pupils to take control of their own learning as they can see its purpose and have identified that doing so will have benefits for them as individuals in helping them achieve something they desire. It builds an intrinsic motivation with pupils, which in itself gives them the resilience and independence needed to achieve well, especially when it comes to sticking with the task of seriously revising for tests and exams.

Central to success in this area is creating a climate where everyone involved with the school has the highest of expectations. Peter Matthew's 2009 Ofsted publication provides an excellent illustration of how even in challenging circumstances schools are able to raise the aspirations of the young people they serve. Of course, this isn't easy. The role of leadership within a school is central to creating a climate and culture where there are no ceilings on pupil achievement and where the educational opportunities provided include chances to develop a wide range of skills such as leadership, team-work, creativity, enterprise and entrepreneurial endeavour.

Great schools have at their heart a clear view of pedagogy that allows for the development of thinking skills and provides appropriate challenge for pupils. As Robin Alexander in his 2004 work on dialogic teaching points out, the development of language through the provision of meaningful opportunities to discuss and debate is critical in developing pupils' abilities to synthesise and process information. The idea of a consistent pedagogy across a school is explored further in Topic 17.

Providing time within the curriculum for pupils to reflect and take risks is not only important for the staff of the school. It is also essential for pupils to develop their own capacity to think for themselves, come up with innovative solutions to problems and express their feelings. Nowhere is this opportunity better exemplified than in the provision of high quality extra-curricular activities that are made available for all pupils regardless of their ability to pay. The very best schools we have learned about have well-developed opportunities for pupils to travel and undertake the very widest range of cultural, geographical and physical experiences as well as to encounter a range of visiting speakers from all walks of life. If schools, particularly those working in challenging circumstances, are serious about creating aspiration, then it makes sense to show young people what is out there and allow them to form their own goals for the future.

In a similar way, most of the schools we heard from at our termly G2G conferences mentioned the systems and procedures in place that enabled their pupils to develop self-discipline when managing their own behaviour. If one of the key features underpinning a great school is a deeply rooted and strongly held set of values among all pupils and staff, then developing a behaviour policy which focuses on the positive and allows young people to make choices and decisions needs to be at the heart of how a climate for learning is established.

These schools have managed to create an environment, partly as a result of the first class teaching available, where pupils are comfortable with their place in the system and can trust the adults they work with to treat them fairly and compassionately, while at the same time maintaining the very highest of expectations around personal conduct. Of course, for many young people there are times when their own personal circumstances can make this very difficult. In such situations, the best schools will have high quality intervention and support available to enable the individuals concerned to develop appropriate strategies and build the capacity to deal with these challenges when they emerge. This commitment to an inclusive approach is again one of the features of the very best schools that allows for the whole learning community to feel a part of the school.

Creating a sense within the school of a shared purpose is important here too. Staff, pupils and parents need to have a clear idea about what the school is trying to achieve and why. Great schools are about creating an ethos that is focused on a joint endeavour, a shared journey to a destination that everyone recognises. How schools achieve this is complex. It is about clarity of aims. It is shaped through every single interaction between staff, pupils and parents. It is about the large set-piece assemblies and open evenings. But it is also about the individual daily dialogue that staff have with pupils and parents. It is about pupils being clear about their own personal goals, and what their next steps are. It is about pupils really understanding that the school is there for them and is helping them to fulfil their ambitions. Central to this is the school's role in setting achievable academic and personal targets with pupils and reviewing them with parents on a regular basis.

Key points

- Does the *link* between aspiration, motivation and independent learning resonate in your context? Have you developed a *consistent* pedagogy that allows the development of thinking skills?
- Is taking *personal responsibility* for making the right choices at the heart of your behaviour management systems?
- Are extra-curricular opportunities well planned and available to all pupils as part of the drive to *raise aspiration?*

Topic 16

Decision-making

A good decision is based on
knowledge and not on numbers.
Plato

School leaders at all levels are making decisions every day. Some of those decisions are made almost without thinking. We rely on our intuition and experience to just know what we need to do. Daniel Kahneman in his great book *Thinking fast and slow* (2011) calls these types of decisions 'system one' decisions. These are the decisions you take automatically. When you turn around because there has been a loud bang behind you, you are doing it instinctively. You aren't consciously thinking 'I wonder what that is; let's have a look'.

The second type of decision-making process Kahneman identifies – 'system two' – is more rational. This is when you stop, take a moment to consider the situation, weigh up your options and then decide. Figure 25 summarises these two different approaches.

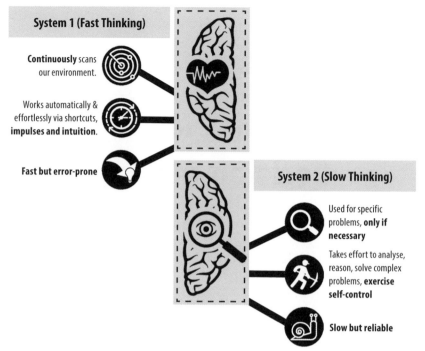

Figure 25: System one and two decision-making
Kahneman (2011)

Understanding your decision-making bias

An important element of system two thinking is making the right decisions on the basis of the available evidence. So, if you systematically and routinely take this into account, taking decisions should be straightforward. The trouble is, it's not that simple. There are various reasons why we don't take logical decisions, even when we try to! Psychologists point to a number of factors than can influence us without us even knowing. Figure 26 summarises the most common types of decision-making bias we all have the potential to demonstrate.

Bias	Definition
Anchoring	The tendency to rely too heavily, or 'anchor', on a past reference or on one trait or piece of information when making decisions.
Availability heuristic	Estimating what is more likely by what is more available in memory, which is biased toward vivid, unusual, or emotionally charged examples.
Endowment effect	The fact that people often demand much more to give up an object than they would be willing to pay to acquire it. Also connected with the 'status quo' bias.
Framing effect	Drawing different conclusions from the same information, depending on how that information is presented.
Gambler's fallacy	The tendency to think that future probabilities are altered by past events, when in reality they are unchanged.
Group think	Peer pressure to conform to the opinions held by the group.
Optimism	The tendency to be over-optimistic, over-estimating favourable and pleasing outcomes.

Figure 26: Common types of decision-making bias
Source: Q-Learning (2014)

Research has indicated that bias tends to operate more in certain situations than others. Knowing when you are inherently more likely to be subject to an unconscious bias can help reduce the chances of this happening. Figure 27 summarises the three most common situations when bias is likely to kick in.

When there is lots of information
- ✓ We notice or think of memorable items
- ✓ We notice when things have changed
- ✓ We remember the things we like

When there isn't much information
- ✓ We create patterns or simplify even when there is little data
- ✓ We fill in the gaps with our stereotypes
- ✓ We tend to focus on the things we know about or like more

When we need to act fast
- ✓ We are over-confident
- ✓ We favour things that we do can straight away
- ✓ We stick to what we're familiar with

Figure 27: When does bias tend to occur?

When it comes to taking good decisions, I have come up with the very simple STOP model outlined below. If leaders just take a moment to stop and think about any given decision and run through the four stages of STOP, however briefly, it can help increase the chances of making the right decision.

The STOP model

Situation
Have you properly understood the situation? What additional information would it be useful to acquire before you make a decision?

Temptations
What is the potential to make a biased decision? In particular, how are you making sure you aren't making a decision based on an emotional response?

Options
What are your options? Take some time to think through other ideas, not just doing the first thing you think of. What else could you do?

Plan
This could be as simple as a short to-do list or a more complex plan, depending what is involved.

Using STOP can help you be less impulsive and more rational. However, the model doesn't mean you should ignore your intuition. Your gut feeling can often help you make difficult decisions as part of a properly considered process. I would argue that the very best decisions are taken on the basis of a good slug of logic combined with a dash of intuition.

Key points

- What is your balance between system one and system two decision-making?
- How well do you limit the potential for your decisions to be biased?
- Might the STOP model be a useful tool for you or a colleague?

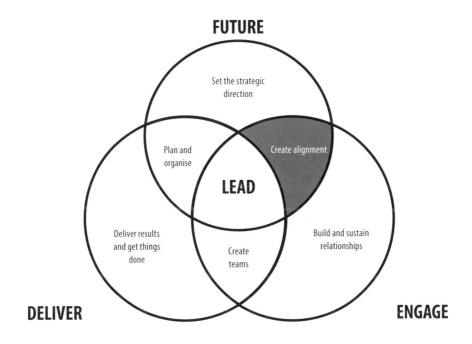

FUTURE

Set the strategic
direction

Plan and
organise

Create alignment

LEAD

Deliver results
and get things
done

Create
teams

Build and sustain
relationships

DELIVER

ENGAGE

Create alignment

Setting an example is not the main means of influencing others; it is the only means.
Albert Einstein

As I mentioned in Topic 1, you can have a great group of staff that are really motivated and love their jobs, but if they aren't pulling together in pursuit of a set of shared goals and with a shared strategy, you won't achieve much. That's why alignment matters so much for leaders at every level. How you achieve this will, of course, depend on your context. But however you achieve it, having a clear set of strategies that underpin the culture you want to create and a group of people who have bought in to that approach is at the heart of great delivery in schools.

There are several things you can do to create alignment within your staff team, and the following topics will examine some of those ideas. At the heart of alignment is great communication, which is of course about clarity of message but also about listening and observing carefully. It is therefore important to remember that communication is a two-way process; it's not just about what you say but equally importantly, what you hear and observe.

Topic 17

Clarity

I continue to be drawn to clarity and simplicity. 'Less is more' remains my mantra.
Stephane Rolland

At the heart of creating clarity is great communication, whether that is in set-piece events or in everyday conversations. The best school leaders continually reinforce their expectations, and talk about them at every opportunity. They continually show staff that they value and appreciate the contribution an individual may be making.

On a day-to-day basis, when these leaders are walking around school they are looking for things to praise and comment on, both with pupils and staff. The odd passing comment can mean a great deal to the individuals concerned and they can go on to have a better day as a result.

It also reinforces to others what matters and what is important. This drip-feeding of expectations as part of everyday interactions can be very powerful.

Sometimes it is the quiet word to one side that is most effective, particularly if one knows the person doesn't like receiving praise publicly. For others, it is the public thanks at weekly briefing that is most important. Again, this not only motivates the individual concerned but also sends a message to other colleagues about what is important and valued.

However, the most powerful way to praise is often through writing to colleagues. A handwritten note to someone, a copy to go on their personnel file, shows that a school leader has taken the time and seen it as important to sit down and make a point of doing something personal.

In terms of motivating staff and gaining their loyalty, the use of a personal note is probably one of the most effective ways of using praise to communicate and reinforce expectations.

When I reflect back to my time in school, there are a number of areas where I think clarity of purpose is particularly important. Some of these are covered elsewhere in this book, but two in particular deserve further exploration in this topic. The first is teaching and learning, which should of course be at the heart of the work of any school. The second is clarity on systems around behaviour and climate for learning.

Clarity of pedagogy

What the most successful schools have done is make sure that every child has a teaching experience that promotes the best possible learning outcomes right across the curriculum, regardless of which teacher they have. They have also managed, by and large, to ensure the job of the teacher is manageable. To achieve this, schools have often undertaken an internal debate: Should our school have an overall pedagogical framework?

This is not an easy question to answer. The first part of the debate centres on whether it is desirable to have a shared whole-school approach to pedagogy in the first place. Some would argue that teachers should be free to develop their own approaches to teaching. After all, most teachers have their preferred default teaching methods which probably reflect how they were taught themselves, their initial teacher training and possibly their own preferred way of learning (which often leads to an unconscious tendency to assume that others learn in the same way). Shouldn't the teacher be allowed to concentrate on these areas of strength? By allowing teachers the professional freedom to plan and deliver lessons in their own way, the assumption is that the quality of teaching and learning will be higher.

This may be true to a certain extent, but many successful schools have recognised a number of problems with this approach. Firstly, the quality of planning and resourcing that one teacher can bring to the range of classes they teach is a limiting factor in itself, particularly if there is an expectation that they are supposed to be putting in place an individualised programme in order to meet the needs of each pupil. Put simply, the task is unmanageable. There are just too many classes, and too much planning and preparation necessary to create the outstanding lessons needed on a consistent basis. This individualised approach also ignores the fact that there may be ways to teach particular skills or knowledge sets that may not be reflected in the individual teacher's repertoire or own experience. In these circumstances there are two possible outcomes: either teachers feel overworked, disenchanted and leave the profession, or they start to cut corners in the name of self-preservation. Clearly, neither of these outcomes is desirable, and certainly don't lead to the creation of the great schools this publication is all about.

What these schools have done is recognise that it makes much more sense for teachers to work together collaboratively to produce high quality schemes of work for everyone to use. This planning also needs to take a realistic and evidence-based approach to meeting individual pupil need. Not only does this bring obvious benefits in terms of sharing the workload, it means the quality of teaching and learning will be based on lessons that are planned around a shared view of the best way to teach something. It also provides the opportunity for those teachers to meet after something has been delivered, share their reflections on what went well and what didn't and make alterations.

To make this shared planning most effective, the best schools have developed a clear view of what makes good teaching. This again presents schools with a major challenge. Any teacher will tell you how fast prevailing pedagogical fashions can change. For example, the debate between child-centred or whole-class teaching is always on the agenda, as is the skills versus knowledge debate. In my view, these are often false dichotomies. Great teaching will involve both great explanation and modelling by teachers who have excellent subject and curriculum knowledge, as well as opportunities for pupils to deepen their understanding and be able to recall what they have learned in a sophisticated and meaningful way.

Then there are practical considerations, particularly as we know teacher retention will always be a key issue. The most successful schools have recognised that teachers are not superhuman. The leaders of the very best schools do all they can to make the teacher's job as manageable as possible, recognising time constraints and practical classroom issues. But at the same time, they make sure that what is created gives teachers the best chance to meet the needs of all their pupils. As a result, some schools have now set out their broad approach to pedagogy very clearly. Doing so has provided these schools with the opportunity to frame planning around a shared approach that is flexible enough to meet the needs of all the pupils, play to individual teacher's strengths and allow the different approaches that the range of subjects need. This approach is about creating a framework, not a straitjacket. It provides a pedagogical bedrock upon which pupil and teacher creativity, experimentation and individuality can thrive.

For example, some schools I have worked with recently have highly developed policy and practice on assessment for learning that has originated from the seminal work of Dylan Wiliam and Paul Black (1998). Another had focused on the importance of developing learning through quality dialogue as described by Robin Alexander (2004) in his work on dialogic teaching. One school has developed a simple summary of what a good lesson looks like. In another, where consistently delivered high quality teaching is at the heart of its approach, every classroom has the teaching framework on the wall. Both staff and pupils know and understand what is expected, and this helps ensure clarity and consistency from all.

Whatever the origins, the benefits for staff and pupils in schools that have a shared pedagogical approach cannot be underestimated. Not only do teachers have the security of knowing they are working in a collaborative way with their colleagues, even those in other subject disciplines, but pupils too can benefit from developing their own sense of how they fit into the pedagogical approaches as individual learners. As we will see in later topics, priority given to developing staff and pupils is a key feature of the most successful schools, and the clarity a shared pedagogy can bring can be of great benefit in helping to achieve this.

Clarity that creates a positive climate for learning

The second area of focus in this topic is around how great schools achieve clarity about the way all staff ought to work together with the pupils to promote a consistent approach to management of behaviour and the creation of a positive climate for learning. In his 2009 Ofsted publication, Peter Matthews describes how the outstanding schools he studied had all developed highly effective behaviour policies and were all absolutely clear about the importance of never assuming for one minute that the job of maintaining the right climate for learning is ever finished.

As can be seen in the very best schools, the equation is simple: in schools with good behaviour, pupils learn more effectively. As well as the obvious direct link between attitudes to learning and learning outcomes, there is another very important factor to consider. The recruitment and retention of good staff is absolutely essential, and schools where staff spend too much of their day trying to maintain discipline are not as effective in attracting and keeping the best teachers and support staff. If good staff leave, then the school can soon find itself on the reverse journey away from its intended destination.

In the most successful schools, all staff play a role in promoting and maintaining a positive learning environment, where good behaviour is encouraged and rewarded, and poor behaviour is appropriately punished. Effective behaviour management is underpinned by clarity, clear systems and shared understanding.

The biggest challenge for school leaders lies in the process through which one translates these aspirations into the reality of daily life in a school. In great schools a clear message emerges time and time again: make sure your behaviour policy focuses upon pupils accepting responsibility for their own behaviour and learning. Support your pupils in developing self-discipline based upon mutual respect, clear boundaries and maintaining faith in a clear and consistent system. Key to this expectation is the need for staff to develop the correct skills and attitudes to manage behaviour effectively.

Creating a sense within a school of a shared purpose is, as we have already mentioned, very important. Staff, pupils and parents need to have a clear idea about what your school is trying to achieve and why. Of course, a well-developed pedagogy is an important part of the equation. If lessons are interesting, well-paced and meet the pupils' needs, then those pupils are far more likely to respond appropriately. However, there are times when the maintenance of a positive climate for learning sometimes needs more than just good teaching. Everyone needs to have a clear understanding of the school's expectations.

A lack of clarity can lead to conflict, because each party makes different assumptions about what is acceptable and what is not. This inevitably means that you need to develop a series of routines and procedures that cover all aspects of school life. Of course, armed with this long list of policies there is always the danger that the school community becomes overwhelmed by the sheer volume of rules and regulations. The very best schools get the balance right.

One way around this is to have a set of generic principles that underpin the way the school operates. The notion of mutual respect is as good a place to start as any. The key question is: where do we draw the line between what is and what isn't acceptable? My own experience has taught me that pupils will always nudge their way up to the line wherever it is placed. What the very best schools do is put the line somewhere that says to pupils, parents and teachers at the school that it expects only the highest of standards. These schools fight any battles in this territory. There is nothing more effective than this setting of the highest of expectations and sticking to them in every aspect of the work of the school.

The evidence has shown that once the overall expectations have been agreed, great schools then break these down into more specific areas. For example, using a series of levels to define positive and negative behaviours, then setting out how a school should respond to them, can create clarity around how situations should be dealt with. Increasingly, I have seen the number of levels within classroom management protocols reducing in schools I work with. In other words, there is a faster escalation of consequences.

One could be forgiven for thinking that clarity around pedagogy and behaviour management systems ought to be a prerequisite of good schools and therefore, given the remit of this publication, maybe not the business of a book looking at what leaders at all levels do to create great schools. However, a common thread running through so many great schools we heard from on the G2G programme, supported by much reading, is that it is the clarity of these systems and expectations that allows schools the security to take risks and experiment, understanding that these journeys into the unknown are underpinned by the solid foundations clear systems can bring.

The very best schools are highly creative both in developing classroom practice and in the way that they encourage pupils to experiment and express themselves freely, often exposing themselves emotionally to their peers. Creativity can flourish when the right preconditions are in place that make pupils feel comfortable and supported. These schools will trial new processes and ideas, safe in the knowledge that business as usual will continue as a result of the hard work that has gone into creating a shared way of working which is understood by the whole school community.

Clarity for groups of schools

In a former role, I had the privilege to work alongside Jon Coles and a team of fantastic colleagues at the United Learning group of schools. One of the things we worked to create was clarity in what we stood for as a learning community. Part of this was articulating the values that underpinned the 'why' of what we did as well as the key strategic approaches of the 'how'.

The first of these was set out in a collection of group values that were created through consultation with pupils and staff from all the schools and the central team. The values listed below provide a strong basis upon which to make key decisions and develop key behaviours.

- **Ambition** – to achieve the best for ourselves and others
- **Confidence** – to have the courage of our convictions and to take risks in the right cause
- **Creativity** – to imagine possibilities and make them real
- **Respect** – for ourselves and others in all that we do

- **Enthusiasm** – to seek opportunity, find what is good and pursue talents and interests
- **Determination** – to overcome obstacles and reach success

Sitting alongside these are the key approaches that define the strategic approach of the group as shown in Figure 28. Known as the United Learning Framework for Excellence, it aims to give clarity and a sense of distinctiveness to the work of the schools, while retaining a degree of flexibility within each school to reflect its unique context and priorities.

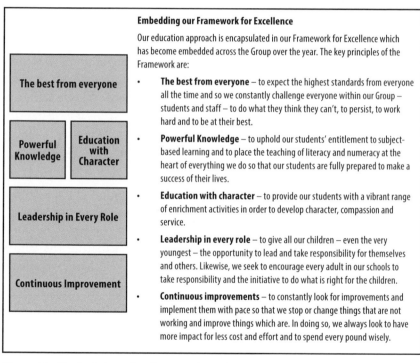

Embedding our Framework for Excellence

Our education approach is encapsulated in our Framework for Excellence which has become embedded across the Group over the year. The key principles of the Framework are:

- **The best from everyone** – to expect the highest standards from everyone all the time and so we constantly challenge everyone within our Group – students and staff – to do what they think they can't, to persist, to work hard and to be at their best.
- **Powerful Knowledge** – to uphold our students' entitlement to subject-based learning and to place the teaching of literacy and numeracy at the heart of everything we do so that our students are fully prepared to make a success of their lives.
- **Education with character** – to provide our students with a vibrant range of enrichment activities in order to develop character, compassion and service.
- **Leadership in every role** – to give all our children – even the very youngest – the opportunity to lead and take responsibility for themselves and others. Likewise, we seek to encourage every adult in our schools to take responsibility and the initiative to do what is right for the children.
- **Continuous improvements** – to constantly look for improvements and implement them with pace so that we stop or change things that are not working and improve things which are. In doing so, we always look to have more impact for less cost and effort and to spend every pound wisely.

Figure 28: Clarity brings freedom to take risks and experiment

Key points

- Do you take time to keep your messages simple and listen and observe carefully?
- Do you need to develop a clear pedagogical approach?
- Do you have clear systems and procedures in place to manage behaviour effectively, thus creating a positive climate for learning?
- Do you need to consider your approach to creating greater clarity in settings that extend beyond one school?

Topic 18

Influencing others

You can never really live anyone else's
life, not even your child's. The influence
you exert is through your own life,
and what you've become yourself.
Eleanor Roosevelt

If creating alignment is all about getting buy-in from colleagues, whatever your role, then being able to influence colleagues is an essential element in any leader's armoury. The previous topic focused on the importance of creating clarity, which is a good starting point.

Engaging others in creating the vision and strategy

If you have the time, it usually well worth designing a process that enables all interested parties to have a stake in helping to shape your vision and strategy. If people have had a say in determining where you want to go and how you might get there together, there is a much greater chance they will deliver their own part of the plan when it comes to making things happen, and more importantly, happen to a high standard. In some ways, this is actually more relevant in schools than it is in some other workplaces, simply because teachers are so often operating solo. Even in schools where people are popping in and out of lessons, teachers are often left to their own devices for much of their working day. In these circumstances, people need to be intrinsically motivated to do a great job as there is usually no one else there checking up on them who can offer the extrinsic carrot or stick.

Inspiring others

But people need to feel more than just consulted. All leaders need to offer inspiration to the teams they lead. It is a critical part of what you need to do if you are to achieve your goals and have the impact for pupils you are seeking. First and foremost, people will be inspired by your passion and commitment. So modelling what you expect others to do, to a high standard and with energy, is a great way to influence others and gain alignment. Setting a good example is a great way to get buy-in.

There are a number of subtle ways you can inspire others. Valuing others' contributions, particularly when they demonstrate discretionary effort or particularly effective performance will inspire. Inspiration is as important in daily communication just as much as at the 'key moments' like the first team meeting in September. If a group of staff trust you and feel inspired by you, they will usually do as they are asked, no matter what they feel about what has been suggested. On the other hand, you can have the greatest idea in the world, but if you have failed to inspire or argue persuasively, few will deliver for you.

Leaders new to a role can sometimes find themselves working with a group of staff where results have been poor for the last few years, where there is poor teaching and learning and where pupils and staff almost seem to drag their feet as they arrive. It can feel like an impossible task to get to where you want to be. In your head, you can see the brilliant learning environments, inspirational teaching and smart enthusiastic engaged learners, but how do you get everyone to see that vision?

Your ability to communicate and articulate exactly what you want is crucial. Your presentation skills are important, and you need to consider how you come across. It cannot be a jumbled mass of thoughts as this will conceal the key messages. Clearly defined pictures of success and the exact map of how to get there will reassure and motivate your team. Giving yourself a chance to rehearse this sort of presentation privately with someone you trust is a great way to ensure you make the most of these set-piece opportunities.

Presentations are a powerful way to engage each and every person, but consideration should be given to the fact that the same information can be perceived differently by people. As before, knowing your context matters. A well-planned presentation ensures that by the end, each person knows their role in the vision, their part in the team, knows that they are highly valued and knows that they are completing the task for excellent reasons. They know that their team leader has complete confidence in their ability to make a difference. The team is clear about what success looks like and what the timeline expectations are. They feel that they have the capability to complete the task with confidence because their leader believes in them.

Integrity

As Stephen Covey points out in *The Speed of Trust* (2008) it is important that leaders are honest, that they don't try to create false impressions or spin the truth. Not only does this build trust but it supports the creation of transparency and develops a culture where it is okay to talk about things that may not be working as well as they might. It is important in these situations to use simple language to describe things as they are and not to manipulate people or distort the facts.

There can sometimes be a temptation to work to hidden agendas or to keep certain facts or viewpoints from people, sometimes even with their best interests at heart. In this context straight talking can often take courage and this will be explored in Topic 32 on difficult conversations.

There is clear evidence to suggest that schools which make the most progress don't allow issues to be swept under the carpet. They see problems that are openly talked about and shared with individuals and groups as opportunities for improvement. This creates honest dialogue and greater alignment.

How such issues are raised however, is also very important. Care needs to be taken to pitch what is being said appropriately. Put too gently, and the point of what is being said may be lost. Put too bluntly, and any opportunity to change behaviour or move a situation forward may be missed.

Developing the skill to get this balance right is not easy and is another example of where leaders need to not only be very self-aware but also attuned to the needs and situation of those with whom they are communicating. Making the space to step back and reflect in these circumstances is also important. Too often the temptation is to rush into a conversation without really thinking through what will be most effective.

Influencing others

You are, like anyone in a leadership role, completely reliant upon other people to get the job done. For this reason, your ability to influence others is crucial. Not only do you need to be able to generate enthusiasm and excitement in the things that you want your team to achieve together, you also need to be able to influence others outside the team who may have an indirect influence or impact on your work.

There are a number of reasons this matters. Depending on your role, you may, for example, want to implement a new curriculum for a year group, introduce a new behaviour system for the whole school or establish a new phonics scheme. Each of these will require buy-in from your staff. Of course, you can insist upon individuals implementing whatever you decide you want them to set up, but unless their teams are convinced of the benefits of any change or new approach, one can be sure discretionary effort will be lower and the subsequent impact significantly reduced. Being able to effectively influence members of your team will play a key role in ensuring changes are effectively introduced.

For middle leaders in particular, being able to influence externally is also very important. Take, for example, decisions that others may take that have a direct effect on your team. You may wish to have an influence around decisions being made regarding whole-school systems for rewarding pupil achievement and behaviour. Or you may be keen to influence how teaching assistants are deployed within your key stage or department. Or you may want a say around the construction of the whole-school timetable. In all these cases, decisions are being taken by others, often in your senior leadership team, that will have a direct effect on the work of your team. For this reason alone, it is important that you are able to exert influence when these decisions are taken. Yes, of course your line manager can act as your advocate if needed, but the more you are able to handle these discussions yourself, the better.

Most school leaders are already very good at influencing others. It is a skill that is developed very early in their careers, as it's precisely what they do day-in day-out with the pupils they teach! But taking some time to think more systematically about how you influence others can pay dividends.

Degrees of influence

First of all, you can think though the different degrees of influence you may be able to exert. Those who you directly line manage are to some extent under your control although, as already discussed, getting buy-in from others, even where a command and control approach is possible, is still by far the most effective approach. Then there are those who you can have a direct influence on, but don't directly line manage. If you have a role in co-ordinating literacy across an area or some form of pastoral or achievement role, for example, you may well have a team of individuals where you are not the formal line manager. Then there are those where that influence may be indirect, where your ability to influence is dependent upon someone else. And then there are those who you just need to accept you have no ability to influence whatsoever. Knowing this can save an awful lot of time and wasted energy. In a more senior role, while you have more hierarchical control in theory, it will usually only be indirectly through others that you can exert that influence.

How you approach influencing someone therefore needs to reflect the degree of influence you have. You can clearly afford to be far more assertive and directive with those who are under your control or over whom you have some direct influence. For those where you only have an indirect influence, you will usually need to adopt a subtler and less assertive approach.

Choosing how to influence

But there is another consideration. You need to think about the range of different ways in which you can influence others. Choosing the right approach will depend, once again, upon both the context and the person you are trying to influence. Some situations are best handled with a straightforward and carefully thought through logical argument. In situations where the facts really do speak for themselves and the person you are seeking to influence is attracted to a logical argument, this is clearly going to be the best approach to adopt. However, that knowledge about the person you are seeking to influence is critical because for some people, the logic of an argument could be beaten, for example, by a more values-based pitch into the discussion you're engaging in. Trying to use a logical argument with someone who is approaching an issue from a more emotional perspective is clearly not the best way of successfully influencing their view or decision. You may also want to consider how much you're prepared to negotiate around a particular issue. This is particularly useful in situations where you have something that may be of value to those who you seek to influence. For example, you may have at your disposal financial resource, or you may be able to influence someone else for them. This 'you scratch my back, I'll scratch yours' approach can be a very powerful way of influencing some people. Of course, others may find it rather distasteful and be much more persuaded by an argument that appeals to their sense of moral purpose.

Others can simply be persuaded by passion, energy and enthusiasm for a new idea. These are people who relish change, like to be in the thick of the action, and don't want to spend too long thinking through all the options. A skilful influencer, therefore, will be thinking about the extent of their influence, the context of the issue under discussion, and the likely response from individuals they are trying to persuade. You probably already instinctively take these factors into consideration when persuading others, but taking time to properly think through how you might approach a particular issue is usually time well spent. Taking time to identify those individuals who might be key to influencing others on your behalf is also very useful. Just like with groups of pupils, there will usually be a few of your colleagues whom others tend to look up to or admire, or they might just be very vocal in the staffroom! Either way, in certain circumstances, there is much to be gained by getting these opinion formers around to your way of thinking and allowing them to then do your work for you in influencing others. Of course, this is often far from easy and may well not be appropriate or desirable in many situations.

So, there is a lot you can do, but it's also important for you to know when to stop. Continuing to try to influence people when it is clear that they're not engaging can often be counter-productive and cause others to dig their heels in. It can also mean that, on a future occasion, your ability to influence is diminished. It's a bit of a cliché but losing the battle for the long-term goal of winning the war can be a short-term price that's worth paying.

Key points

- Do you need to engage staff more with shaping vision and strategy so you get greater buy-in?
- Think about the strategies and opportunities you have available to inspire others. Do you always make the most of them?
- What strategies do you use to influence others?
- Are these adjusted to the context or the person?

Topic 19

Managing up

Once you become a victim, you
cease to become a leader.
Annie McKee

When people talk about managing up, they often have some sense that this is about an individual trying to manipulate their boss in some way or even convince them to do something they otherwise wouldn't do! Managing up is therefore seen as somehow slightly dishonest or underhand, but actually, nothing could be further from the truth. Managing up is all about making sure that you have a productive relationship with your line manager that supports both of you to achieve the shared goals for the pupils you both serve. It's about you taking your share of responsibility for the quality of your joint working relationship so you can both work towards mutually agreed goals that are in the best interests of you, your line manager and your school. It isn't political manoeuvring.

The benefits of managing up
If you are good at managing up, you and your manager both stand to benefit in a range of different ways. Not only are you more likely to get the kind of resources that you need, you will also have created a strong working relationship that benefits you both. So, getting that relationship

right is in everyone's interests. Like a great marriage, though, it takes work from both parties!

For middle leaders in particular, having a good relationship with your line manager also gives you a direct route into the senior team of the school. Not only can this lead to improved opportunities for you to gain experience beyond your current role, it is also a good way to help ensure that the members of your own team are on the radar of your senior colleagues. In other words, managing up is all about creating positive, mutually beneficial relationships for you, your team and the organisation as a whole.

So, what does managing up actually involve?
There are a number of practical things you can do to strengthen your relationship with your line manager. First of all, how well aware are you of their expectations of you? Similarly, have you clearly articulated the expectations that you have of them? For example, do you know how your line manager likes to receive information and how often? Do they prefer a regular e-mail update, or are they happy to let you get on with things on the basis that you will only get in touch if there's the something you think they need to know?

In terms of your own needs, have you talked to them about the ways that you like to work and the things that you find energising? Do they know those that can have a negative impact on your effectiveness at work? This is where using simple psychometric tools, such as those we offer at Leadership Matters, can be enormously useful. Beginning to articulate the things that motivate each of you can quickly lead to more productive working relationships. As a line manager yourself, you may want to think about how you can enable these important conversations to happen with those you manage.

Secondly, when you are faced with an issue or concern, making sure you don't just arrive at their door with a problem, but come with possible solutions and ideas about how the problem can be solved is usually welcomed.

Thirdly, if there are issues that are concerning you or if there are disagreements between you and them, it is usually beneficial for you both to try to address these sooner rather than later. It may well be the case that your line manager is blissfully unaware that you have a particular concern or worry. Getting these things out in the open as soon as they arise is beneficial to your relationship in the long-run, and also enables the issues to be dealt with before they become an even bigger problem.

Fourthly, it's important for you to be as honest as you can with your line manager. Their trust in you can very quickly be eroded if they discover you've tried to hide something from them or distort the truth. It's also important to remember that trust is more than just a measure of personal integrity, it's also about someone's view of a person's competence. This means you should think about how you can give your line manager reassurance that you know what you're doing and that you're delivering results. Taking opportunities in meetings with them to present well-organised data and other information combined with good planning and personal organisation will give them confidence that you're on top of the job.

To sum up, when it comes to creating alignment, as the quotation from Albert Einstein earlier reminds us, never underestimate the power of leading by example. If you can demonstrate through your own actions the success of an idea, properly implemented, others will follow. It comes as a surprise to most leaders, whatever role they are undertaking, just how much others notice the things that they do and say. It is no good saying to others that it is important to always challenge pupils if they are shouting in the corridor and then fail to do so as a leader. The old adage that 'it is not what you say but what you do that counts' sums up beautifully how this form of communication is crucial. One's behaviour can either powerfully reinforce expectations or quickly destroy them. This will either build or erode the trust and motivation of colleagues.

For precisely this reason, it is critical that you make sure you really do offer strong exemplification of what you wish others to do. To say one thing and do another is usually extremely dispiriting and is very likely to lead to poor implementation by others.

Key points

- Do you make the time to consciously manage your relationship with your line manager?
- Do you take responsibility for your share of the responsibility to ensure you understand one another's perspective?
- Is your relationship with your line manager characterised by honesty and trust?
- If it's not, what can you do about this?

Topic 20

Inspection and review

Whatever words we utter should be chosen with care for people will hear them and be influenced by them for good or ill.

Buddha

In most school settings there will be a time when someone will come in from outside to judge the quality of the educational experience you are offering and the progress your pupils are making as a result. This is another context where the theme of alignment that underpins this part of the book is important. If these reviews or inspections are to go well, there needs to be a joined-up view of your school's strengths and areas for growth. Leaders at all levels need to be speaking with one voice, with confidence and surety.

That's the goal. The trouble is that many leaders inevitably find such situations pretty stressful. Interviews with inspectors can be daunting and often very competent leaders can perform below par in such situations. One way to help with this is to use a simple framework to help you organise and rehearse your thinking. Figure 29 shows one way this can be organised. You may want to adapt this to suit your setting or context.

Judgement
- Is it outstanding, good, RI or inadequate?
- How secure is the judgement?

Evidence
- What is your evidence for the judgement?
- How has this been validated?

Focus
- What are the current priorities in this area?
- Why are you focusing on these?

Impact
- What has been their impact so far?
- How do you know?

Figure 29: JEFI – a model for aligning thinking during external review

Many of the schools I have worked with over the last few years have used JEFI or something similar and found it a useful way of reducing the risk of that 'rabbit in the headlights' moment that can so easily happen during a review or inspection interview. Some schools have even created the opportunity for staff to practice such interviews with one another. The simple template in Figure 30 is an example of how even minimal preparation can help staff with this. If staff fill in just two or three bullets in each box, schools I have worked with have been struck by how this approach can bring alignment and confidence to what leaders are saying to reviewers.

	J Judgement	E Evidence	F Focus	I Impact
Leadership and management				
Teaching, learning and assessment				
Personal dev, behaviour and welfare				
Outcomes for pupils				

Figure 30: A template for using JEFI

But there is an important health warning here. I am not advocating that inspection becomes the focus for a school and its activities, you will note this book hardly mentions it. Rather, using a simple framework like JEFI can build a confidence that reduces stress and worry and create a sense of preparedness without inspection becoming a dominating feature of a school's culture and climate.

Key points

- Could you make use of a framework like JEFI to bring greater alignment to external reviews or inspections?
- How might you approach introducing this in a way that reduces, not builds, anxiety?

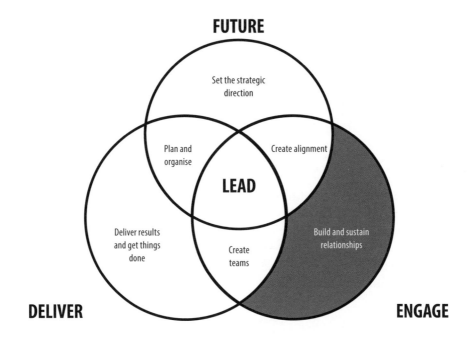

FUTURE

Set the strategic
direction

Plan and
organise

Create alignment

LEAD

Deliver results
and get things
done

Create
teams

Build and sustain
relationships

DELIVER

ENGAGE

Build and sustain relationships

I suppose leadership at one time
meant muscles; but today it means
getting along with people.
Mahatma Gandhi

Building and sustaining relationships is one of the most important elements of any leader's role. As the popular quote attributed to Peter Drucker says: 'Culture eats strategy for breakfast'. Although in my belief he is using culture here as something more akin to culture and climate combined, the point is that you can have the greatest strategy in the world, but if relationships between you and your staff, and among the staff themselves aren't good, then delivery and pupil outcomes won't be what you want them to be.

Topic 21

Transparency and trust

The truth is like the sun. You can shut it out for a time but it ain't goin' away.
Elvis Presley

A number of schools I have worked with that have used Jim Collins' work (2001) have been taken by what he would describe as 'confronting the brutal facts while never losing faith'. These schools are completely transparent in the way they look at themselves, gather data, share and process that information and then draw conclusions about their next steps. They have completely understood the need to establish the truth of a situation in the school in the strong belief that the right decisions will then become self-evident.

As one school puts it: 'If things are not working, we are encouraged to say so. This is underpinned by openness throughout the system, especially in terms of data and accountability. We work hard to keep things transparent, but we try not to use the data or knowledge for blame but as a means to identify and then tackle issues. This has not always been the case but is something that has evolved as our leadership has become more confident on the reliability of our data.'

Using data and other information to monitor the performance of pupils, individual staff and any team as a whole, is a key part of any leader's role. However such a system is established, it needs to be understood by all staff and not just seen as an accountability tool for the senior team of the school. Of course, accountability is important. There will always be the need for leaders at all levels to ensure that their staff are performing well, and that solid evidence exists to make judgements about colleagues' effectiveness. However, for each team to become truly reflective, there also has to be a strong professional trust that centres on the information needed to bring about change for the better: better for your pupils, better for your staff and better for your whole school community.

How leaders use data and information

The whole-school systems you put in place need to be evidence-based and evaluative. Schools regularly collect large amounts of data but sometimes fail to use this wealth of information to properly track individual pupil progress, the progress of specific groups or indeed the progress of pupils overall. The critical condition for success is to create a culture of openness where this information is shared and used not just as a way to judge progress, but also to help the team as a whole, as well as the individuals within it, to develop as professionals.

Thinking about your own team, you need to consider how much of the data that relates to each team member is shared and available to the whole team? Do you create opportunities for your team to use your data to help identify individual and team areas to both celebrate and improve on?

Keeping faith

Hopefully your data will tell a story of improvement over time, but this won't always be the case. How you respond to information that paints a less than rosy picture is really important. It can be very tempting for you to bury bad news and carry on in the hope that things will get better. Sometimes they do; but by not embracing bad news and using it as a way to learn and improve, an opportunity is missed. To paraphrase Jim Collins (2001), the best organisations will always 'confront the brutal facts but keep the faith that something can be done'.

Creating a climate where transparency pervades all of a team's activity is not easy. However, there are a number of practices that you can adopt to support this. Firstly, you can ensure that when you are debating and discussing issues as a team, it is the merit of a particular argument, grounded in data and evidence, that is the basis for decision-making, not the force of personality. This could be a discussion about the best way to teach something or how to set up a whole-school initiative on literacy. Using data and other evidence to support the decision-making process depersonalises the arguments and usually leads to better decisions being reached.

Secondly, when things go wrong, examination of the underlying reasons needs to be conducted in a 'no-blame' way. This is about you creating a climate where experimentation and learning from mistakes is encouraged. For example, if an idea to introduce lunchtime catch-up classes doesn't seem to be having the impact you had hoped for, or if the change of syllabus you have introduced in your own department or one you line manage hasn't led the increase in results you had anticipated, what is needed is an approach of 'What went wrong and how can we work together to improve the situation?' rather than 'Whose bad idea was it to do that?' Once again, the focus is not on who is responsible for a particular situation having arisen, but what the facts of the matter are that the team can learn from.

Thirdly, you need to make sure that there is an openness in the way decisions are made and communicated. When you are allocating resources, deciding who works with which groups of pupils or how work is allocated among the team, try to work to an agreed set of principles that everyone can see are being fairly applied. Nothing is more divisive than colleagues thinking that a leader, at any level, has favourites or hidden agendas when it comes to making appointments for example, or writing the timetable.

Responding to unwelcome news

Paradoxically, a charismatic leader can sometimes work against creating a culture of transparency. A strong leader, who everyone wants to please, may be exactly the kind of person to whom it is very difficult to bring bad news. Hearing that behaviour is becoming a bit of a concern, for example, can sometimes be the last thing a leader wants someone to tell them, even though they know it is important. Of course, how you as a leader respond to challenging information brought to you by an individual is important.

If you give a defensive or irritated response, this will obviously tend to deter someone from raising issues again. But equally unhelpful is if your response where challenging information is received involves you taking no action. In either case, it is unlikely that person will bring up difficult issues again.

To sum up, highly successful teams operate in a climate and culture where information, data and decision-making are shared openly and used supportively. These teams have 100% confidence in their own ability to bring about the changes needed. In other words, they keep faith in their own capacity to overcome difficulties even in challenging circumstances. This resilience and inner strength comes from a sense of common purpose and collaborative endeavour supported by strong and highly effective leadership that inspires the necessary confidence and self-belief.

The importance of trust

Collaboration and partnership are words commonly heard in schools. While these are crucial elements of any school's success, it is probably true to say that many educationalists talk about partnership working and co-operation without really taking time to consider the conditions that allow for such effective practice to take place or what it actually looks like on the ground.

It is vital not to overlook the importance of creating a climate of trust where you are able to concentrate your energies and talents reaching your goals, rather than spending time engaged in unproductive and misdirected activity associated with concerns about others' motives and unnecessary bureaucracy.

In his book *The Speed of Trust*, Stephen Covey (2008) sets out why building trust is so important for the success of any organisation. In his view, where levels of trust are low, staff will be working in an unproductive environment which is sometimes associated with unrest and where they are often divided into political camps. It's an environment where bureaucracy slows down productivity and creates low levels of innovation and development. Inevitably, discretionary effort is low.

In teams with a high level of trust, systems and procedures are helpfully aligned and bureaucracy is kept to a minimum. Individuals are trusted and supported to carry out their work. There are positive and transparent relationships among staff, leading to innovation, confidence and loyalty, and discretionary effort is high.

How do you build trust as a leader?

As Covey helpfully suggests, there are just two key elements to building people's trust in you.

Firstly, people need to trust your character. They need to know you have faith in them and care about their success as individuals. Finding ways, through the use of praise and feedback, to let people know when you think they are doing a great job is the easiest way to do this. They also need to know they can trust your integrity. Do you respect others' confidences when they share personal or sensitive information? Do you avoid over-promising, so you can always do what you say you are going to do, even when this is difficult? Do you treat everyone fairly?

Secondly, and often overlooked, do others have trust in your competence and judgement? Your staff need to be confident you know what you are doing, even if inside you don't always feel like you do! One easy step, however, is to lead by example on things you are asking others to do. Not only is this an excellent way to influence others, it helps create the culture of 'how we do things around here' as well as building their confidence in your ability to deliver. I am not advocating you do this all the time, but it is a powerful way of building trust. It is also important to make sure you regularly reflect on your strengths and weakness as a leader and work systematically and consistently on building those areas of strength as well as addressing those where you need to improve.

Figure 31 is a useful summary of the key elements that Stephen Covey believes underpin a leader's ability to build trust.

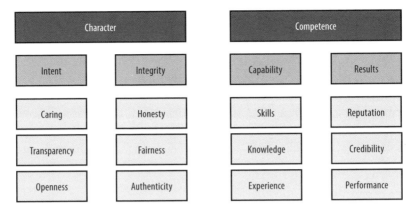

Figure 31: The key elements of trust
Adapted from Stephen Covey's *The Speed of Trust* (2008)

Exemplifying trust is an important symbol

Some of the examples that follow may appear to be somewhat simplistic, but they do demonstrate – in a very straightforward way – where institutions have high levels of trust.

Teams with a high level of trust will not have systems and procedures that are about always checking up on people. For example, if the head of a curriculum area requires their team to submit their lesson plans to them on a daily basis, their team is likely to feel that the quality of their work and the level of their professionalism is in question. This is in no way to undermine the importance of the support that new entrants into the profession will need with lesson planning. Nor is it suggesting that peer-to-peer sharing of ideas is unhelpful. Where trust is undermined is where there is an implicit suggestion that someone cannot be trusted to complete work to an appropriate standard unless it is going to be checked.

Schools where the locking of doors is deemed unnecessary by staff show a high level of basic trust between all staff and pupils. Of course, there will be times when this trust is undermined by a particular individual, but a school that has the confidence in itself and all the people who work there to leave doors unlocked sends a clear message to everyone. Not only that, but the time wasted when someone needs to enter a space that is locked and they don't have the key is a classic example where a lack of trust can slow up proceedings and reduce productivity, motivation and effectiveness.

Another key indicator of a high trust school relates to processes for delegation, which are examined in more detail in Topic 26. Clearly, good leaders will often delegate tasks, but to maintain high levels of trust, it is essential that once something has been delegated, the person concerned is left to carry out the task they have been given. It can often be tempting to ask or advise a colleague about what is being done throughout the process. This can actually create more work overall, make the person feel undervalued or not trusted, and is generally unproductive.

In low-risk situations, it is sometimes better to allow a colleague to fail to complete a given task satisfactorily and then go back through it afterwards. The learning that can emerge is often far more powerful than if there had been an earlier intervention. Of course, if the person doesn't have the necessary skills or experience to cope with the task they have been delegated then they are unfortunately being set up to fail. Part of the skill of a good school leader is knowing when it is the right time to delegate, making sure that colleagues know they can ask for advice if they need to without any negative value judgement being made about their abilities.

Trusting pupils

For leaders in a pastoral role, showing your pupils you trust them is very powerful, although the principle applies in all contexts. For example, giving your pupil or pupil council a proper remit to consider issues that go beyond school dinners or the toilets is important. Do they have the chance to help you appoint staff? Are they trusted to input on financial decisions? Some schools give councils a small budget with which they can prioritise areas for spending. What other leadership roles do you create for pupils? If you have a curriculum responsibility, how much do you seek and trust the views of pupils about the quality of provision? In both primary and secondary phases, pupils can be surprisingly astute when it comes to making judgements about the quality of the deal they are getting.

The speed of trust

Finally, it is just worth considering how quickly trust can be built and how quickly it can be destroyed. Interestingly, Stephen Covey suggests this isn't the same for each of the elements.

When it comes to people trusting competence, this can be established pretty quickly. In a modest way, you can discretely make others aware of your track record. If you have been promoted internally this may not even be necessary. You can also ensure some quick wins which make everyone feel confident that you know what you are doing. This element of trust is also usually slow to decline. People tend to cut you a bit of slack in the short term if something goes wrong, although you clearly need to make sure this doesn't become too regular an event!

When it comes to your personal integrity however, precisely the opposite is true. It can take a while for people to know they can trust you to keep confidences, for examples. This aspect usually needs testing before your colleagues will trust you; they need to know from experience. Conversely, your integrity can be destroyed in an instant if you are found to have been dishonest about something or gossiped about something private. Keeping this in mind is critical, as for some people, if this happens it can mean they will never trust you again.

Showing loyalty

We have already talked about the fact that all schools and individuals can face challenges and difficult times. What good leaders appear to do in these circumstances is keep faith with the individuals that make the school successful. There is a clear link here with developing a 'no-blame' culture. Just because someone has made a mistake with the timetable or said something inappropriate to a pupil or parent, doesn't mean leaders should suddenly forget the important contribution that they make. In fact, quite the reverse is usually true. In these situations, what staff need to know is that they are supported and trusted and that they can be relied upon to learn from their mistake and move forward.

In contrast, when things are going well, the very best leaders generously give credit to all those who have enabled that success to happen. There is nothing more disheartening and likely to reduce trust than for an individual to see a leader take credit for something someone else did. Openly acknowledging the contribution of others is critical.

Loyal leaders will also speak up for an individual even when they may not be present and even if it may be uncomfortable to do so. Rest assured, word will get back and the person concerned will feel even more valued and motivated than they did before. This, in turn, builds momentum and alignment towards the school's goals.

Loyal leaders also resist the temptation to 'bad-mouth' colleagues behind their backs. As mentioned previously, they respect the individual concerned by dealing with them directly and raising any concerns they may have face-to-face. They don't say: 'I'm not saying anything I wouldn't say to them myself.' They keep such matters private, however tempting it may be to talk about the issues.

So, to summarise, building trust has a significant impact on the culture and climate of any team. There are three key elements for you to keep in mind: showing faith and care for the success of others; your own personal integrity; and your perceived competence and track record.

Key points
- How open are you with data and other information?
- How good are you at confronting the brutal facts but keeping faith in your ability to overcome them?
- How could you find out about perceived levels of trust from your teams?
- If you identify there is a need to build trust, what are the actions you might undertake as a priority?
- Do you show respect for everyone you work with, regardless of their role?
- Are you loyal to colleagues, even when it is difficult to be so?

Topic 22

Little things matter

We sometimes underestimate the influence of the little things
Charles W. Chesnutt

Stephen Covey (2008) is very clear about how the best leaders genuinely care for others and are naturally happy to show that they care in an open way. They respect the dignity of all staff members no matter what their role in the school. Taking time to have a conversation with the caretaker who has a bad back during exam season is just as important as comforting a deputy head who may have suffered a personal loss.

School leaders who take the time and trouble to do something to support a colleague, or who take a personal interest in a particular pupil who is dealing with some really tough problems at home, send a clear message to the whole school community that people matter to them. You can so easily become so embroiled with your own problems on a day-to-day basis that you forget how important it is to get these things right.

Sending a card wishing someone well or organising some flowers to be sent takes a few minutes to put in place but can mean so much to the person concerned. But taking this trouble does more than just support that individual. The message that colleagues matter as people and not just as employees permeates the whole institution. That buys loyalty and commitment. It reinforces the ethos that staff and pupils are valued. It makes the school a place that people are proud to belong to, and proud to be a part of.

The cumulative effect of many small acts of kindness is immeasurable. The little things that leaders do can build morale and a sense of trust, and play a significant role in developing momentum. If people feel valued and cared for they reflect that by valuing and caring for the place they work in and the people they work for.

If you also model that behaviour to pupils, they in turn gain greater trust in you and a sense of belonging to their school. It is a very simple, virtuous cycle that leaders need to remind themselves of frequently, particularly during times of stress when it becomes far more likely that the importance of respect and dignity might be overlooked.

Many of the best schools I have worked with also make important statements about how they value their staff more generally. For example, some of these schools provide free tea and coffee in the staffroom at break-time, even though pressures on budgets are always tight. Others offer a free lunch for those staff sitting with pupils at lunchtime or who are running a club. These gestures are highly symbolic and represent a powerful way of building momentum and helping create a climate where people naturally begin to act in a self-disciplined way because they feel valued.

In one school, the senior team goes to great lengths to ensure staff are, in their words, cherished. This doesn't look the same for everyone. The school believes it is vital that the senior team carefully works out a personalised plan for each member of staff which ensures that they feel valued and nurtured. Part of this involves ensuring every exceptional deed is personally recognised by the head.

The same school also ensures that relaxation is valued. Monday breakfasts, Friday cakes, fruit bowls and chocolates delivered to offices, end of term celebrations, social events, prizes and celebrations for attendance, great practice and team spirit are all part of the mix. The head even says to the staff 'if you hear of anything another school does that means that they care more, then tell us and we will do it!'

Keeping reflective and creating time to think

In Topics 11 and 12, we explored the issue of developing people. Part of this analysis includes an acknowledgement of the importance of creating a culture where your staff are constantly learning on the job. School leaders are no different and should take the opportunity to model this behaviour and lead by example.

Having a reflective approach to the job and a willingness to listen to colleagues is critical. Remembering the importance of asking the right questions rather than being expected to know the answers fits with this approach.

Many school leaders I coach find this a very useful way to support the process of reflection. Having quality time set aside, supported by someone with the right skills, can often make a real difference in helping leaders think through complex challenges.

An appreciation of the importance of learning about the personalities of those we manage is also helpful. While it is important not to overplay this, it is again useful to employ some flexibility around how you manage different individuals. For example, most schools have members of staff who are natural followers of systems and procedures but sometimes find it hard to see the bigger picture. They can easily become obsessed with the most unimportant of scenarios, even becoming quite stressed.

Compare this with those individuals who are great at thinking out-of-the-box but have a much more laissez-faire approach to certain situations which can undermine and frustrate colleagues when they don't follow school procedures properly. Both types of colleague require a response, but the nature of that response should reflect what school leaders have learned about the individuals concerned, and in particular their different personalities.

In general terms however, the important thing is that school leaders don't stop reflecting or learning. You look after your own personal and professional development and you make time to step back and see the bigger picture.

Your relationship with governors

Leaders in schools often reduce their capacity to think in a strategic way because they don't give themselves time to think, reflect and grow as leaders. The best leaders I work with have understood this and don't feel guilty about making quality time to reflect. If you are a head or system leader, investing time in building your relationship with your governors or trustees can be an effective way to step back and take the strategic view. Your relationship with your chair has the potential to be particularly useful in this regard. Having the opportunity to build an open, honest and trusting relationship with your chair will allow for healthy debate, challenge and recognition, all of which will make you more effective. Apart from anything else, it helps reduce that sense that it's 'lonely at the top'.

Day-to-day behaviours

My own experience and working with thousands of school leaders over the years has taught me that none of us realises the impact of our own day-to-day personal behaviours and organisational skills. For example, there is nothing more frustrating for colleagues than leaders who:

- don't reply to a letter or e-mail within a day or two of it being sent
- regularly turn up late to teach or to meetings because they have been dealing with 'more important' matters
- leave colleagues out of the loop regarding a particular issue or event
- forget to do things that they said they would do or even do something differently from that which had been previously agreed
- ask for feedback at the end of an event and then fail to act upon it or even acknowledge the feedback the next time the event is organised
- don't meet deadlines that all staff are expected to meet
- make (often poor) decisions 'on the hoof' because they have failed to plan ahead effectively.

Not only do badly organised leaders have a direct negative impact on the areas they are managing, they also have an impact on leadership capacity more widely. Their ability to inspire and motivate is diminished, they don't have the same level of credibility with colleagues and morale is inevitably lower. Staff start to feel disenchanted and question why they should go the extra mile when their line manager doesn't appear to value them. Of course, most of the time, nothing could be further from the truth. School leaders do value their colleagues, it's just that the implicit messages caused by poor organisational skills might suggest that the focus on personal performance needs to be increased.

When things do go wrong the best leaders are up front in saying so. They take responsibility for not delivering and talk about what they need to do differently in the future. This openness helps to build trust and transparency. There is more that might help you reflect on your personal organisation and effectiveness in Topic 36.

Not forgetting to have some fun!

Schools can often be stressful places. External expectations seem to grow every year. Staff and pupils seem to work increasingly long hours in pursuit of their goals. In such circumstances, it can be easy to forget the importance of having fun. Seeing the funny side of difficult situations, playing the odd harmless practical joke or just remembering not to take everything too seriously is essential.

For school leaders this principle can operate on two levels. Firstly, it can permeate all their everyday interactions. Clearly there are some leaders for whom this will be easier than for others, but cracking a joke or making a witty comment is the bread and butter of some of the best leaders at all levels.

However, this can't be about individuals trying to be something that they're not. Keeping a frame of mind where one tries to raise a smile can be important in lifting spirits and making work a more fun place to be, but it needs to be genuine and heartfelt. You need to be true to yourself but give yourself permission to have a bit of fun now and again.

Secondly, schools need to plan for plenty of occasions where staff can socialise together and enjoy themselves in a more relaxed environment.

It is a chance for you to show your staff team that they are valued and respected, but it is also another way to build relationships and make sure people have fun together. Of course, this can be organised by middle leaders in sub-teams as well as by more senior staff for whole-school events.

The dividend earned from investing resources in providing for some special occasions can be huge. It builds trust, momentum and a sense of well-being, all of which build a school's capacity to develop its people.

Key points

- Do you show staff you care about them through the little things you do?
- How regularly do you do this? Do you need to systematise this in any way?
- Do you make time to have some fun?

Topic 23

Managing conflict

When team members trust each other and know that everyone is capable of admitting when they're wrong, then conflict becomes nothing more than the pursuit of truth or the best possible answer.

Patrick Lencioni

Within wider partnerships and your own team, if a key part of your role is to build and sustain relationships, there are inevitably times when you have to step in to manage conflict. While conflict is usually something that has negative consequences, it can also be a productive way to move a situation forward if handled carefully. And of course, as we explore in Topic 25, constructive conflict where individuals are able to debate a point without it becoming personal, is an essential feature of high-performing teams.

But there are times when conflict can be debilitating. It can arise in a whole range of different ways and with people from outside your team as well as those from within. Conflict often arises because of resourcing issues, for example someone may have a disagreement with a colleague about how much funding a particular course needs to run successfully; or they may be unhappy about the progress the pupils taught by a particular teacher are making. Conflict can also arise because of disagreements about who should be doing what. A lack of clarity on roles within your team can lead to people vying for position, particularly if they are manoeuvring themselves for promotion or other recognition. A classic example is when there are two people who are both organising the same thing, such as an assembly or a meeting agenda or an important whole-school initiative, where neither wants to cede ownership of the project.

How should you respond to conflict?

First of all, it is important to appreciate that context is the critical factor here. Taking time to reflect on the type of conflict is an important first step. Is the disagreement a result of resource, a power-struggle, a difference in values or a personality clash? Or is there something else at play? Working this out first can usually be very helpful in deciding how to manage the situation.

In doing this, you need to avoiding making too many assumptions about people's motivations. In working out the best way to handle a situation, it is usually well worth having conversations with the individuals concerned to try to understand their positions more accurately.

It is also important for you to know yourself well. We all have ways in which we tend to respond in conflict situations, usually without really being aware of this. Taking time to reflect on this can also be helpful, as we all have to guard against the tendency to just dive in to try to solve a problem using the same old strategy, regardless of the context.

Choosing the right strategy

Kilmann's 1974 model of conflict management in Figure 32 sets out five ways you can respond to or manage conflict.

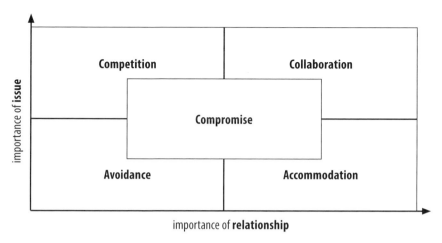

Figure 32: Five approaches to managing conflict
Thomas Kilmann (1974)

In each case, there is a different blend of the extent to which the response meets the needs (and tackles the issue), as opposed to the needs of the person or people one is in conflict with (and giving greater importance to maintaining relationships).

For example, if your sense of the situation is such that someone in a team is attempting to test your authority in some way, for whatever reason, you may decide the appropriate response is to entirely focus on meeting your own needs and pay no regard to their perspective. Such an approach is often known as 'forcing' or 'competition'. In this situation you will firmly pursue your concern despite any resistance from the other person. This type of approach has the advantage of usually providing a quick resolution to conflict or disagreement and can establish your authority not only with the individual concerned but also with the team or staff as a whole. However, taking this approach can sometimes cause the other person to react even more negatively and you need to be prepared to deal with that. It goes without saying, however, that these sorts of conversations are usually best had privately.

In contrast, there can be occasions when it is actually much better to completely back down from a position and concede on the issue being discussed. This can often be a useful tactic when the issue means more to others than it does to you, while giving you the opportunity to demonstrate that you can be reasonable, listen to arguments presented and not just assume that you are always right. This approach is sometimes known as 'accommodation' or 'smoothing'. If used too often, however, you runs the risk that your supporters may start to lose faith in your authority or ability to take decisions. Once again, you need to use your own professional judgement about when it is right to back down on an issue.

There are some areas of conflict however, like choosing a syllabus or curriculum or designing an assessment system, where you would ideally like to find a way forward that all parties are happy with but that doesn't compromise you core beliefs. This 'win-win' approach, or 'collaboration', is a chance to come to a mutually beneficial result in which the underlying concerns of all parties have been met. This approach usually takes time and requires a high level of trust between all involved so that you can work through any feelings of animosity. It has the benefit, if carried out successfully, that you gain a reputation for being a successful negotiator. In addition, you build mutual trust and respect with and between your staff, and a shared sense of ownership. However, this approach can be very time-consuming and may not be practical when a quick solution or fast response is required. And it doesn't always work. Again, you need to make a judgement about whether going for a collaborative approach is worth the effort.

Another way to respond to a conflict is to simply ignore it! This is known as 'avoidance' or 'withdrawing'. This can be appropriate if the issue is trivial and simply not worth the effort or when there are other more pressing issues that need to be dealt with. Sometimes you may wish to simply postpone a response because it is not the right time or place to confront a particular issue. This approach can also buy you some time before deciding how to respond. On the other hand, you need to be aware that supporters in your team can see avoiding a particular conflict as a sign of weakness. Using withdrawing strategies without negatively affecting your own position does require skill and experience. The fifth approach to managing conflict sits right in the middle of each of the four already mentioned and is unsurprisingly called 'compromise'.

Compromising looks for a mutually acceptable solution that partially satisfies all or both conflicting parties. Again, you will need to make the call in the context of your particular situation about whether accepting a compromise is the right way forward. It can often be a first step to building trust with staff and usually has the advantage of quickly resolving the situation. It can also be useful when taking the more extreme positions of withdrawing or forcing the issue are judged to be unlikely to work, or too risky or time consuming.

Some of these strategies are easier and more tempting than others, particularly if you are new in post. Avoiding an issue or smoothing over can be the path of least resistance, but as the old saying goes, 'there's no pain without gain'. Sometimes you just need to have the courage to do the right thing.

Key points

- When you are faced with a conflict situation, do you take time to properly understand the different perspectives of those involved?

- Does Kilmann's model offer a useful way of thinking about the different strategies available for approaching conflict situations?

Topic 24

External partnerships

The best partnerships aren't dependent
on a mere common goal but on a
shared path of equality, desire, and
no small amount of passion.
Sarah MacLean

Great schools are not islands, they see themselves as having a role that extends beyond the walls of their own their own institutions. This not only includes the support they provide for their immediate local community, it also encompasses wider support for other schools in the system. For schools that operate within a wider group of schools, this ought to be one of the advantages of such arrangements, and these schools acknowledge the benefits that this outreach work brings for themselves. Linked to this, as a school leader, you are very clear about the fact that you don't have the answers to all questions and are constantly seeking to improve and innovate by learning from others outside your own immediate context.

Setting up relationships with leaders in other schools isn't easy and takes time. There are sometimes local tensions that arise from competition for pupils, or even staff, that make it even more difficult. But where mutual benefit can be derived, there is a growing body of evidence which shows it is worth school leaders spending time to build relationships with other schools both informally and as part of more formal collaborations such as teaching school alliances, trusts or other networks. In any inter-school collaboration, it is important to not just drift into these relationships.

There are some key questions to consider:

- What is the shared purpose for the partnership? What is the driver?
- What is the partnership aiming to actually do?
- What does the leadership of the partnership look like and where does it come from?
- What are the boundaries of the partnership and what is the governance?
- How does the partnership fit within the wider context and other partnerships?

When it comes to reviewing how well your partnership is working, whether that be as part of a formal group of schools or as a looser alliance or network, you might also find the work of David Hargreaves (2011) useful. He has created what is effectively an audit tool for school partnerships. You can access this resource via LM Insight on the Leadership Matters website or through the reference section at the end of this book. Figure 33 is my attempt at summarising his thinking.

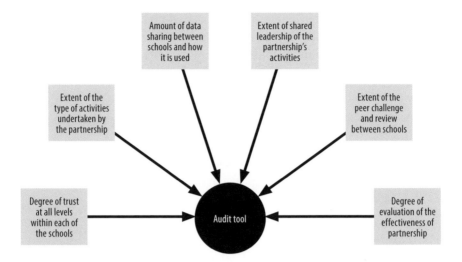

Figure 33: Auditing your partnership

Based on a think-piece by David Hargreaves (2011)

For many years the debate around school improvement has included a discussion about whether a top-down or bottom-up approach brings the greatest level of success. Early on it was clear that top-down approaches on their own don't work. While there was clear evidence that in many circumstances bottom-up improvement was more successful, the results are inevitably inconsistent with some areas both within and between schools failing to reach acceptable standards of performance.

The concept of lateral leadership is based on peer-to-peer support either within a single school context or between two or more schools working together. With a growing number teaching school alliances and academy trusts complementing pre-existing networks, there are many opportunities for this type of collaboration. Often based around a coaching model, the approach allows for individuals to take responsibility for their own learning while at the same time having appropriate levels of challenge from a professional colleague. This approach is not limited to senior or middle leaders but can be applied at all levels within the teaching and support staff of any school.

One school I know has worked hard to create a climate where risk taking is encouraged. Great lessons are photographed, described and shared via Twitter or whole-staff emails. There are signs used saying 'I am taking a risk' which can go on classroom doors if staff are being extra-creative and worried whether an approach will work or not. The most effective teachers are trained as peer coaches and the school uses 'learning three' teams as part of its teacher development programme for newly qualified staff. These teams consist of one teacher in their first, second and third year of teaching. Many schools, building on the concept of working in threes, are now using a 'lesson study' approach to professional development.

Key to the success of any self-improvement, particularly in the context of lateral leadership, is the notion of appreciative enquiry. The best schools take the view that it is always better to build on perceived and actual strengths than simply concentrate on the problems that need solving. This approach recognises that it is important to create an environment where it is okay to try out new ideas and is based on a credit not deficit model of school improvement.

One word of caution. Schools need to be rigorous in the way they define outstanding practice before they share it. Too often, one can fall into the trap of recycling mediocre practice rather than genuinely effective and innovative ways of working. To do this requires a culture of honest feedback where the trust between individuals and schools enables this to happen and where taking an evidence-based approach, as we discussed previously, is at the heart of your strategy.

Formal groups of schools

In the English educational system, a key change over the last few years has been the emergence of multi-academy trusts (MATs). These are groups of schools that are no longer part of a local authority group of schools and have instead joined together as a single independent trust. The table below summarises a set of findings in relation to what appears to make these trusts most effective. While the report from Ofsted (House of Commons, 2017) focused on MATs, I have no doubt these conclusions would equally apply to charter schools in the United States or other similar examples that may emerge elsewhere.

✓ An ability to recruit and retain powerful and authoritative executive leaders, with a clear vision for bringing about higher standards

✓ A well-planned, broad and balanced curriculum that equips pupils with a strong command of the basics of English and mathematics, as well as the confidence, ambition and team-work skills to succeed in later life

✓ A commitment to provide a high-quality education for all pupils, in a calm and scholarly atmosphere

✓ Investment in professional development of teachers and the sharing of knowledge and expertise across a strong network of constituent schools

✓ A high priority given to initial teacher training and leadership development to secure a pipeline of future talent

✓ Clear frameworks of governance, accountability and delegation

✓ Effective use of assessment information to identify, escalate and tackle problems quickly

✓ A cautious and considered approach to expansion

Figure 34: Features of effective multi-academy trusts
House of Commons (2017)

When it comes to making time and space to think strategically, one great way to do this is through working with other schools. When leaders at any level have the opportunity to meet colleagues from other institutions, not only do they learn a lot from each other, but they inevitably reflect on their own context from a slightly different viewpoint.

Key points

- To what extent do you engage with or enable productive partnerships with other schools?
- In Hargreaves' audit model, what are your areas of strength?
- What might be potential areas for growth worth investing in?
- Is there anything in the Ofsted summary of recommendations on what makes successful MATs that is useful in your context?

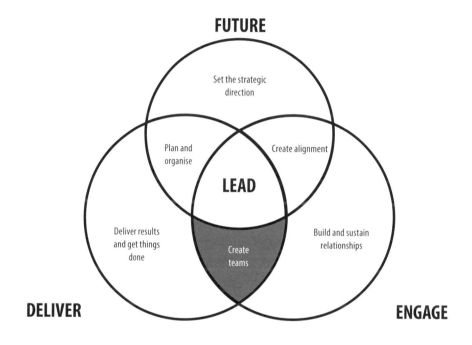

Create teams

I'm going to tell you the story about the geese that fly 5000 miles from Canada to France. They fly in V-formation but the second ones don't fly. They're the subs for the first ones. And then the second ones take over – so it's teamwork.
Sir Alex Ferguson

As a school leader, at whatever level, you will probably be working with a diverse range of individuals. Some of your staff may well be very experienced, extremely confident and need very little support and guidance from you. These individuals have a huge amount to give to the team as a whole. Bringing out the best in your high performers is vital, particularly as the temptation is to focus on those staff who are much less experienced, much less confident and look to you for support and guidance.

Some of your staff may be very aware of their own strengths and weaknesses, whereas others may lack the self-awareness that enables them to see themselves as others do. Some team members may be facing significant external pressures from family or other aspects in their lives. Some may be highly ambitious individuals; others may be very content with their current role and have no plans to take the next career step.

So that's straightforward then! Your role is to help support these disparate groups of individuals and shape them into high performing teams committed to a shared vision, in a way that brings out the best in each of them. What follows is a summary of some things that can help.

Topic 25

Teams and teamwork

Alone we can do so little; together we can do so much.
Helen Keller

When thinking about teams and teamwork, it's probably worth just taking a moment to think about what we mean by a team. The very best definition I have come across is from Katzenbach and Smith (2003):

'... a small group of people with complementary skills who are committed to a common purpose, performance goals and approach for which they are mutually accountable.'

It's a powerful set of ideas. For your own team, how true are the different elements within this definition?

- Is it the right size?
- Do you have a good blend of skills, experience and expertise?
- Do you care about the same things – is your purpose the same
- Separate from this, has everyone bought into the performance goals you are working towards? Does everyone know what they are?
- Do you have an agreed high level strategy that you all believe in?

- Do all members of the team hold one another to account, not just the leader?

How well does your team work together?

While ensuring that you are able to make the most of your formal meeting time, taking time out from the day-to-day pressures of your role to reflect upon how your team is working together as a unit can be very productive.

Much has been written about how such high performing teams develop. We all know this doesn't happen overnight and that most teams go through a series of stages before they are really effective. The most well-known model for describing team development was created by Bruce Tuckman (1965), and is summarised by his four stages of *forming, storming, norming* and *performing.* There is a simple logic to his analysis that definitely resonates in a school context. We can all probably think of a team that never got beyond the internal politics and jockeying for position that characterises the storming phase of a team's development. It is interesting to note that Tuckman suggests trust doesn't appear until the final stage of his model. He would argue that trust takes time to build and is the product of how the team has built relationships over time.

But a more recent model developed by Patrick Lencioni (2002), suggests that for a team to develop, trust needs to be there at the very beginning. Without trust, he would argue, team members can't properly debate and argue without it becoming personal, which results in superficial discussion and challenge that leads to poor decision-making and performance. As with Tuckman, this is also a pretty compelling analysis.

A team model for schools

So who is right? Well in a sense, they both are. If we combine the two, we have a model that starts at the beginning with the formation of a team and goes on to show how a team can, using the trust that has built up, go on to enjoy powerful debate and a shared sense of buy-in into the team's goals as well as the programmes needed to achieve them. In other words, trust is somewhere along the journey, not at the start or the end.

Figure 35: A model for team development

Formation
Early days; getting to know each other; lots of saying the right thing; not rocking the boat; OK but superficial relationships.

Adjustment
Personal views are asserted; people vying for position; lots of assumptions about motives; misunderstanding and bad feeling is not uncommon; difficult time for the leader to manage.

Trust
Trust between team members is developing; they are comfortable in exposing their own worries, fears, vulnerabilities and weaknesses; they are honest with one another; people feel valued, supported and respected by others in the team.

Debate
Team members trust one another enough to be able to disagree and argue about decisions and issues without it being personal; the focus is doing the right thing, discovering the truth, not winning an argument.

Buy-in
There is genuine buy-in and a strong sense of commitment from all team members when key decisions are taken, even if there has been earlier disagreement, because all ideas and views have been properly considered.

Performance
Team members, not just the leader, do not hesitate to hold one another to account for their behaviours and adherence to decisions and standards; there is a shared sense of ownership of the whole team's goals; the team are acting as a single unit and performing highly.

Having a framework can really help a team reflect on how it works together. With all the day-to-day pressures of leading in a school, teams can be forgiven for sometimes finding it hard to find time to review strategic goals and progress towards them. It is even harder to devote valuable time to stepping back and reflecting on how well your team is actually functioning. Yet, if Henry Ford is right, doing so is critical. To be moving forward together effectively, the senior team needs to be working in a way that harnesses the strengths and talents of everyone in the team and challenges itself to be even better.

And just like a Model T Ford, there need to be periodic checks of all the vital components; its oil filter and brake pads need renewing from time to time. Senior teams are no different. They can benefit from a simple diagnostic check and, just like cars, can benefit from the renewal of some of the basic elements that ensure smooth running. Using a model of team development can be one useful way of diagnosing how well your team is working. But finding time to use this analysis to then improve upon ways of working as well as re-charging team relationships out of the work environment is also important.

Developing leadership talent

Within the wider context of developing your staff, another thing that great schools are good at is identifying and nurturing talent. Whatever level of leadership you are currently working at, you have the opportunity to spot future middle and senior leaders among those you are working with. Apart from the obvious benefits for succession planning within your own school or group of schools, we all have a responsibility to develop the pipeline of school leaders across the country. Great schools have systematic programmes of leadership development in place to do just this. As well as opportunities for learning about leadership in theory, critical elements of these programmes include the chance to take on new roles and experiences, work-shadow and have coach or mentor support. I have worked within a number of groups of schools to help them do just this across more than one school, which opens up a whole range of other exciting opportunities.

But there are some things we need to be better at in this regard. I still don't think we are good enough at recognising the inherent unconscious bias we all have, myself included, that tends to see 'potential' as looking like us! By recruiting and developing staff according to the norms that already exist, we run the risk that future leaders will continue to be dominated by white males, who some would argue, may have a tendency to lead in a certain way. When I talk about knowing and understanding the strengths and talents of others in your team in Topic 11, it is important to remember that different leaders bring different strengths. Not everyone should conform to a certain view of what a leader looks like. In one school's senior leadership team I worked with recently, where the head had been in place for a number of years and appointed pretty much the whole team, 90% of his colleagues had identical personality profiles. He had appointed in his own image!

We also need to make it easier, for women in particular (but not exclusively), to combine the challenges and pressures of working as a school leader with family life. Again, this requires heads and system leaders to think more creatively and differently about how they can be more flexible in the way things are organised within schools.

Recruitment

Great teams, just like great schools, don't usually happen by accident. Care and attention is paid to each school's recruitment process. Advertisements are attractive, the interview is thorough and professional, and schools are not afraid to take the decision not to appoint and start over again if a suitable candidate fails to materialise. The more successful the school becomes, the easier it gets and the higher the bar can be raised. Increasingly, great schools and their governing bodies are using professional recruitment services, particularly for more senior appointments.

As Tim Brighouse and David Woods (2008) helpfully point out in *What makes a good school now?* being fussy about appointments is essential, no matter how challenging your recruitment context. They remind us that to 'appoint in haste, or when not entirely sure, is to repent at leisure'.

By the same token, you may need to be prepared to take a risk by overstaffing if a particular recruitment process produces two outstanding candidates for a post. Clearly financial constraints mean this is not possible in all circumstances, but in core subjects particularly, there is evidence to show this approach pays dividends in the longer term.

When one of the primary schools I used to work with needed to appoint an assistant headteacher, the candidates that were finally short-listed were each so good that the school appointed all three, despite the short-term impact on the budget. As a result, the school had three excellent class teachers as well as three highly effective senior leaders who worked together to help the school become outstanding.

Another school appointed three very suitable PE candidates when only one permanent post was available. The skill set and attitude of the individuals was such that they adapted and were supported to be highly successful in alternative shortage fields. The school then supported those colleagues in taking the step back into their area of specialism when the right time came.

Thinking back to what builds discretionary effort, staff appointed need to fit with your school or group's core values. The recruitment process needs to assess whether the person is aware of the vision and shares in the values that underpin your work and has a genuine passion for the job on offer. One school we heard from asks potential candidates to read the school's pedagogical summary online and then asks questions at interview based on the document. Such an approach not only tests their understanding of good teaching but also says something about their self-motivation, organisational skills and how much they want to work in your school.

If you want to delegate to others more, you need to have people who are able to work without being tightly managed and while they may need to be guided, led and taught, they are not constantly supervised. If too much time is spent on motivating and monitoring a colleague, the situation rapidly becomes mutually unproductive. The right people will be largely self-motivating and self-disciplined, compulsively driven to do the best they can.

Effective colleagues will also demonstrate a genuinely mature team approach to their work. For example, when things are going well they will identify those people who have contributed to that success. When there has been a problem they will take responsibility rather than blame others.

The very best schools also take time to consider what balance is needed within any given team. One of the outstanding schools I have worked with uses the *StrengthsFinder* system when appointing staff. As well as watching teachers teach as part of the recruitment process, they ask prospective staff to undertake a *StrengthsFinder* questionnaire to better understand what individuals have to offer and how they will complement the needs of a particular team. They then use this knowledge to ensure that staff are given roles which play to their strengths. Using this approach has also given the school a common language when discussing the strengths or weaknesses of its work.

Retention

Great teams need stability. To retain good staff it is important to make sure achievements are recognised, that working conditions are good, that staff can see progression in their career and that staffing structures are flexible enough to allow this to happen. More generally, there is no substitute for making sure that everything comes together to make the ethos of the school as positive and energetic as possible. Topic 2 focuses specifically on what leaders can do to build discretionary effort, this sense of engagement. People like to work in a place that feels good about itself.

Indeed, such schools tend to have a generally more stable staff, running contrary to the common view that a good turnover of staff is necessary to bring in new experience and to provide opportunities for professional development.

As Peter Matthews in his Ofsted publication *Twelve outstanding secondary schools* (2009) points out, if teachers are good then heads will seek to retain them by providing new challenges, responsibilities and experience within the same school.

This lower staff turnover means it is easier for schools to maintain consistency in the way procedures and systems are followed. It also helps to foster strong relationships between the staff and pupils and promotes the previously mentioned strong team-based approach to embedding the deep-rooted culture within a school.

One head I know believes staff turnover is low partly because of the in-house professional development and the opportunities provided for staff to take on temporary responsibilities. The school has developed its own web-based 'me and my career' model for staff, which suggests activities and training at each stage in a teacher's career. Staff can complete the activities at their own pace and are then well placed for promotion.

Key points

- How well does your team match the definition given at the start of this topic?
- Where are you on the team development model?
- What might be a useful focus to help you and colleagues become even more effective?
- How much attention do you give to developing talent, recruitment and retention? What more could you do?

Topic 26

Delegation

From a young age, I learned to focus on the things I was good at and delegate to others what I was not good at. That's how Virgin is run. Fantastic people throughout the Virgin Group run our businesses, allowing me to think creatively and strategically.

Richard Branson

The job of any school leader is never done. Your to-do list just seems to keep getting longer. The scale of the pressures and expectations never seem to diminish. Of course one can add to that the pressure you usually place yourself under to do everything to a high standard, on time, and in a way that makes the biggest difference for your pupils.

There are no easy answers to resolving some of these tensions. However, the effective use of delegation can not only help you relieve some of the pressures that you find yourself under, it can also empower, enable and support members of your team to develop or take their next professional step. When done well, delegation is a virtuous circle where all parties feel engaged, trusted and have a reasonably decent work-life balance.

Making delegation work

It isn't easy. When it comes to giving someone else in your team responsibility for writing a particular scheme of work, for example, or leading on a whole-school attendance initiative, there's always that nagging doubt in the back of your mind that you could probably do the job quicker and better than the person you are thinking of delegating it to! On the other hand, failing to delegate effectively to members of your team can leave your staff with the feeling that they're given insufficient responsibility or that when they are, your inability to resist the temptation to micromanage makes them feel undervalued and distrusted. There is another challenge that needs to be carefully considered. Some leaders in schools that delegate frequently can run the risk of being perceived to have abdicated their responsibilities. They are seen as simply passing jobs on just to get them off their desk. So it's important to make sure that when you delegate, others do not have that sense of abdication, but instead feel empowered and trusted.

So what makes for effective delegation?

First of all, you need to always consider what you're delegating and why you're delegating it. Are you delegating to get rid of work you just don't like or to develop someone? Secondly, to be a good delegator you need to be able to let go; you can't continue to control everything. You should hand over to other people those tasks that are stopping you from reaching your full potential because you're trying to do too much. The model from The Hay Group (2007) in Figure 36 shows the three elements that need to be in place for successful delegation.

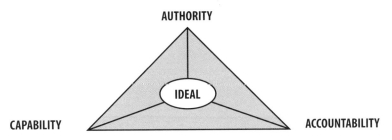

Figure 36: The three key elements needed for delegation
Hay Group (2007)

People can be most effective as leaders, and are most likely to take responsibility, when three things are in place:

- They have the *capability* they need, which includes skills and resources.
- They have the *authority* to act, to be an acknowledged decision maker in that field.
- They are also *accountable* for acting.

Providing two out of three is not enough, however:

- Accountability and authority without capability leaves a leader exposed, unable to do what is expected of them.
- Capability and accountability without authority leaves a leader undermined, constantly second-guessed and over-ruled.
- Capability and authority without accountability means the leader is sheltered from responsibility, which is potentially bad for the organisation.

This can often be useful to create a delegation plan. Some people find it helpful to create a matrix that shows members of a team, the main things the team is trying to achieve and the skills and experience each individual is gaining. Through this transparent approach, you will be showing the whole team that you are keen to enable a fair and even distribution of responsibilities, as well as ensure that each of them has a chance to take on new challenges and develop professionally.

Making sure that you have a good process of delegation is also very important. You need to make sure that a particular task is suitable for delegation and that it can be successfully achieved by the person that you're delegating to. It is completely counter-productive for you to delegate a task that either needs your input, or is beyond the current capabilities and skills of the person you're attempting to delegate to. In either case, to delegate such a task is unfair on your team member and in the long run probably will cause you more work! Linked to this, it's important to be clear what the task is that is being delegated and what is in its scope and what isn't. People like to have clarity about what's expected of them, so they can do a good job and not disappoint.

Linking delegation to performance development can also be very powerful. If in discussions with your team, you can identify a particular development area for each team member, you have a very positive way in to delegating tasks that will help those individuals build the skills and experience they are seeking to develop. As the earlier topic on alignment pointed out, when it comes to motivating and influencing others, it's important for you to put yourself in the position of the other person and understand their internal motivations and personal drivers. If when delegating, you're able to align what you need to have done with what people are looking to develop, you have created the classic win-win situation. That is why looking at delegation in the round and considering the needs of all your team when drawing up your delegation plan has such potential. Working in this way, you are able to create the best fit across the whole of your team.

Also linked to developing the performance of your team is making sure that, together, you take time to identify any particular training needs. If you're asking one of the team, for example, to take a lead on data across the team or at a whole-school level, then it may well be the case that some training in the use of data or the software systems used in your school will be helpful.

You might also want to consider providing coaching or mentoring support for members of your team. This could be provided by other members of the team, from elsewhere in the school or even from beyond the school. However it is achieved, when individuals are taking on new challenges it can be really helpful to have the support and guidance of someone who is not part of the direct line management chain to help them get to grips with what they are facing.

A framework for delegation

When delegating tasks, it's important to be flexible about how the delegation will work in practice. In this context it can be very helpful to use a delegation framework to identify the precise degree to which one is delegating. For example, when taking a decision, does someone you're delegating to need to ask you for permission, ask for your advice and then decide or just tell you what they have done after the event?

There is a very simple framework that describes nine clear levels of delegation where level one represents no delegation whatsoever and level nine is, in effect, fully distributed leadership.

1. Look into this problem. Give me all the facts. I will decide what to do.
2. Let me know the alternatives available, with the pros and cons of each. I will decide what to select.
3. Let me know the criteria for your recommendation, which alternatives you have identified and which one appears best to you, with any risk identified. I will make the decision.
4. Recommend a course of action for my approval.
5. Let me know what you intend to do. Delay action until I approve.
6. Let me know what you intend to do. Do it unless I say not to.
7. Take action. Let me know what you did. Let me know how it turns out.
8. Take action. Communicate with me only if your action is unsuccessful.
9. Take action. No further communication with me is necessary.

Figure 37: The nine levels of delegation
Tim Brighouse (2007)

This framework can be a useful way of agreeing with a member of any team where on the continuum colleagues would like to operate. Of course, the further down the continuum one moves, the greater the degree of trust one needs to show in a team member, and the greater degree of confidence they need to have in themselves to complete the delegated task or role successfully.

As part of agreeing a delegated task or role, it's important to reach agreement on the timeline and any deadlines. You also need to agree how you will know how well the project is progressing. Once this has been done, it can be quite useful to ask the team member to briefly write up what they think has been delegated, how they will take decisions and when they will report back. This is a helpful way of both empowering them to own the task as well as giving you the opportunity to check that they have a shared understanding of what has been agreed.

Finally, it is important for you to let people know how they are doing and if they are achieving their aim. If there are problems, you should try to avoid going into blame mode. Rather, identify what's gone wrong, try to understand together how this has happened and, ideally in a coaching conversation, help the team member to work out what needs to be done differently. That way, the team member continues to feel trusted but at the same time can learn from their experience and improve on their work. It is your responsibility, as the team leader, to absorb the consequences of failure and create the culture where setbacks are an opportunity to learn and grow.

1. When you delegate, make sure the other person is **set up to succeed** because they have the capacity and competence (with support, if needed) to achieve the task.

2. Make sure there is **clarity** about what is required, by when and to what standard. People usually don't know all the detail you have in your head.

3. **Be patient**. Remember that to start with it is unlikely that the person you are delegating to will carry out the task as well or as fast as you would.

4. Don't assume how much the person wants you to keep close to the task. Have a conversation. This will avoid them thinking you are either micro-managing or, at the other extreme, that you have abdicated your responsibility. **Agree with them** the frequency and nature of check-in points.

5. **Don't underestimate** what people are keen or able to take on. Usually people are pleased to be asked, especially if you are playing to people's strengths or stretching them.

6. Make sure the people you delegate to have the **authority and resource** to get the job done. And don't just delegate all the **boring jobs** or those you'd rather not do.

7. Make sure you **plan ahead** and give people plenty of time, rather than using delegation only when you are under pressure for time yourself.

8. Make sure you **don't delegate high risk or critical projects** unless you are 100% sure the person can deliver them. It isn't fair to put someone under that pressure.

9. When you delegate, think about **who else can help** or what the interdependencies of the work might be. Might it be something to delegate to a team rather than a person?

10. Make sure you say **thanks** for a job well done!

Figure 38: Top tips for effective delegation

And when success has been achieved, don't forget how important it is to properly credit whoever is responsible. However you do it, it's important you pass on the credit for success, rather than let others think you have been responsible. Nothing is more dispiriting than for a team to see its leader take the credit for something they didn't do!

Key points
- How well do you delegate?
- What could you do to make your delegation more effective?
- Does the framework for delegation offer a useful way to help with this?

Topic 27

Team meetings

When you go to meetings or auditions
and you fail to prepare, prepare
to fail. It is simple but true.
Paula Abdul

The time you spend together with colleagues is precious and usually quite limited. But it has the potential to support the effective working of a team or, if badly handled, to actually have the reverse effect! In thinking about meetings, it's just as important to remind yourself that often what happens before or after a meeting can sometimes be just as important as the things that actually happen in the meeting.

Before a meeting
First of all, make sure you have a clear process for setting an agenda, prioritising items and clarifying who will lead each item. You need to remember it isn't your job to lead each item. The more others take the lead, the more you will be working as a team rather than as a group of individuals that are doing what they are told. You should aim to make sure each agenda item has a clear time allocation. You should be clear in advance what the outcome required for each item is – for information, discussion, or decision? Ensure you allow sufficient time for people to read papers in advance of the meeting and try to predict which areas for

discussion may need careful handling. It's also a good idea to think about whether any pre-discussions may be appropriate.

During a meeting

At the start of the meeting it can sometimes be helpful for a chair to review the agenda and reprioritise if there seems to be insufficient time to cover all the items. When doing this, they should make sure they think about those items that are important not just those that appear urgent.

You should make sure you have agreed who is going to record any actions from the meeting and who is keeping an eye on timings. Sometimes it makes sense for this to be someone other than the person chairing the meeting. Whoever is chairing the meeting should try to create a climate where everyone has the opportunity to contribute. Sometimes this may mean inviting individuals to make a contribution, particularly if they are less confident, in a way that won't cause undue embarrassment or resentment. But the golden rule is to make sure all your meetings finish on time. This will require the whole team to resist the temptation to go off on a tangent or go into too much operational detail. Often, these discussions can be more effectively considered by a smaller group of individuals outside the meeting. When you feel the time is right, you may want to suggest rotating the chair of meetings. This is a powerful way of showing the whole team that they will have an important role to play as well as giving them the opportunity to develop new skills. At the end of the meeting, if it is helpful, try to take time to review the key actions. Where appropriate, you should agree to the date and time of the next meeting and make sure you finish by thanking all the participants and finish on a positive note, however difficult earlier discussions may have been.

1. Be clear what type of meeting it is – **what is it for?**
2. Make sure the **environment** is right; offer refreshments?
3. Don't have a meeting for the **sake of it**
4. Make sure the **right people** are there; use sub-groups
5. Ensure there is plenty of **notice** of meetings and pre-work
6. Have a **clear agenda** (prioritised; realistic; timed; owned)
7. Agree **meeting protocols** for discussion and stick to them
8. Usually best **not to 'present'** anything – send out pre-reading (in good time) and assume it has been read properly
9. Keep a clear **record** of agreed actions
10. **Chair** should: encourage participation; keep focus; keep to time
11. Mobile technology **protocols** are clear and followed
12. **Rotate** roles of chair and note-taker, where appropriate
13. Clarify **outcomes** at the end and thank everyone
14. Share notes of meeting **promptly**, with actions, owners and timelines
15. Use **pre- and post-meeting** discussions to 'oil the wheels'
16. **Participants** should: listen; respect others' views; be honest; challenge constructively; respect confidentiality; adhere to cabinet responsibility

Figure 39: Top tips for effective meetings

After a meeting

Stress the importance that the note of actions is agreed and circulated promptly. Where there have been particularly sensitive discussions, consider whether a short post-discussion conversation may be appropriate with individuals. From time to time, ask people in the team for feedback. What can you do to improve your meetings?

Meeting protocols

Taking some of these ideas a stage further, one strategy I have seen used successfully in a number of schools is that of developing a meeting protocol for how meetings are conducted, this can be quite prescriptive and amount to what is almost a meeting pedagogy. Figure 40 gives an example of how one of these works in practice.

Before the meeting
1. Have a mechanism to agree two or three **priority items**
2. Circulate a short document that summarises:
    - who is the **owner** of the issue
    - why it is **important**
    - what the owner wants **help with** (*eg* advice for reflection or decision to be made in the meeting)
    - relevant **pre-reading** as background

At the meeting
1. **Brief intro** by owner of the issue
2. Each person, in order, **gives help** asked for
3. Go **round** again
4. **Final** chance for a 'chip in'
5. Owner **summarises** what they are taking away/makes decision

Figure 40: Using a meeting protocol

Getting your meeting structure right

For all leaders, particularly those of you in senior or system leadership roles, one of the challenges can be creating time for strategic discussion. In *The Advantage*, Lencioni (2012) advocates thinking about meetings as being of three distinct types. Figure 41 shows how his approach has been modified by one school to suit their particular context.

Daily (No more than 15 minutes)

- Go round each in turn
- 60 secs **operational** update plus request discussion item
- Agree agenda for short discussion in meeting
- Keep to time (by only briefly discussing priority stuff)

Weekly/fortnightly (No more than 2 hours)

- Clear on purpose/outcome needed in relation to specific **plans**
- Timed and owned
- Papers in advance
- Clarity on how meeting is conducted to ensure max. efficiency
- Agenda next time agreed

Termly (3–6 hours; ideally off-site)

- Same broad approach as for weekly meeting
- But only about creating and/or reviewing **objectives/strategy**

Figure 41: Three types of meeting
Adapted from a model by Lencioni in *The Advantage* (2012)

Developing a collaborative approach

Helping the members of a team work together effectively can often involve spotting opportunities for small sub-groups of your team to work together on particular projects. For example, groups of two or three working on curriculum planning or a specific whole-school initiative, can be a powerful way of building relationships within a team as well as playing to the individual strengths of the team as a whole.

The key to making this work is for you to think through carefully who is likely to work well with whom and in which particular area of work. There's nothing worse than asking two people to work together, particularly at an early stage of developing a collaborative approach, if you're not sure they are currently able to do so well. This also applies if you're delegating a task to a sub-group of the team when they're not confident they have the skills and experience to carry out what is required. This can have the effect of reducing, not increasing, the collaborative spirit within your team.

Challenging in the right way: mind your Ps and Qs!

As we have already seen, great meetings don't just involve you and your colleagues sharing ideas and debating issues. They sometimes involve disagreement or challenge, and this is a healthy feature of a great team. The trick, of course, is for this to not feel personal. It is about the idea or the behaviour not the person. It's about discovering the best way forward, not winning the argument. It's about the good of the team and what is best in the long run for your pupils. Unfortunately, the way in which we sometimes disagree or challenge one another can increase the chances that someone will react defensively.

One way we can minimise the chances of this happening is for us to mind our Ps and Qs! There are various theories about the origin of this phrase, but its meaning is pretty well understood: it's about being polite. So how can this help when it comes to robust debate in a meeting? Figure 42 shows how the Ps and Qs model works.

PRAISE
Positive feedback
Give two or three examples
Be genuine
QUESTION
In a non-judgemental way
Be invitational
Be curious

Figure 42: Minding your Ps and Qs

If you are good at making points in meetings without people getting defensive, you probably already have the habit of focusing on the positive before asking a curious question. Taking this approach is usually much more likely to engender a response that gets colleagues *thinking* rather than *defending*. If you dip into Topic 30, you will see similarities between this model and *feedback tennis*.

Key points

- How well do your meetings operate?
- How do you know?
- Is the structure of your meetings effective?
- Could the stand-up, sit-round, step-back model offer anything useful in your context?
- Might you or any colleagues benefit from minding your Ps and Qs?

Topic 28

1:1 meetings

Tone is often the most important part of
a conversation – and listening is so much
more important than what you say.
Hoda Kotb

Sitting down one-to-one with someone can be powerful. Of course, more formal appraisal and performance management processes are an important element of line management, but the power of the regular, developmental conversation is, in my view, at the heart of what really drives improvement and performance. Taking the time to agree how these conversations will work in practice is in itself an important part of the process. Figure 43 describes some of the features of great 1:1 meetings.

1. Agree or **contract** with one another at the start how your 1:1s will work.
2. **Schedule** your 1:1s well in advance and avoid cancelling.
3. As you delegate more, let your team members each **create their own agenda** (maybe provide an agenda template to help) – add in your items afterwards. Decide if you will settle the agenda **before or in** the meeting.
4. Avoid the temptation for them to be updates – this can often be done in other ways. Try to make your 1:1s about things that need **discussion**.
5. Ask **questions** more than you give advice. Make your 1:1s **developmental**.
6. Occasionally, **ask for help** with something you are working on that you would value their opinion or help with.
7. Make your 1:1s feel **personal**. Ask them how you can do this.
8. Try to ensure they **leave feeling** valued, energised and positive.
9. If you have any follow-up actions, try to do them the **same day** if you can.
10. Occasionally, **ask for feedback** on your own performance.

Figure 43: Top tips for great 1:1 meetings

The key here is to avoid 1:1s being meetings where someone shows up and is just expected to account for themselves and their work. No one looks forward to meetings like this. While this is obviously necessary sometimes, finding other ways to do this can allow colleagues to bring ideas and discussion points to the table feeling empowered and trusted. I often used a quick pro-forma that I sent to my line manager in advance of the meeting to give an update on all the key areas of interest, so we both knew where everything was up to and could then focus on what we really needed to discuss together. An example of a 1:1 update pro-forma is on LM Template.

You may also find it useful for your team to use a personality tool, such as LM Persona to help them understand one another's personalities as a team, as covered earlier in this book. This doesn't just help you better understand the individuals in your team, it also gives your team members a better understanding of you. Some people find the use of these sorts of tools quite threatening, so taking time to talk through how best to introduce such an idea can be helpful.

Key points

- Have you talked with your team about what they would find useful when they are in a 1:1 with you?
- What about your line manager? Do they know what would work well for you?
- How well do you make time for discussion while making sure that all the basics are being done well?
- Might using a 1:1 update pro-forma be a useful way to help with this?

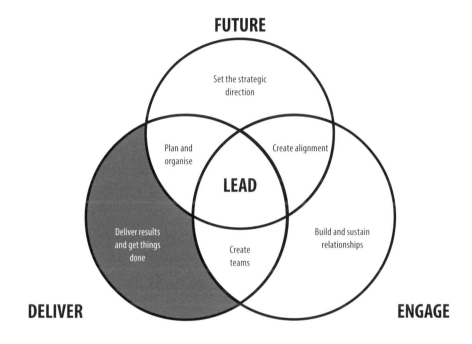

FUTURE

Set the strategic direction

Plan and organise

Create alignment

LEAD

Deliver results and get things done

Create teams

Build and sustain relationships

DELIVER

ENGAGE

Deliver results and get things done

However beautiful the strategy, you should occasionally look at the results.
Winston Churchill

When it comes to the key actions leaders need to undertake, we have so far focused on strategy, alignment, building relationships and creating great teams. All of these are clearly important. But in the end if, as a leader, you don't actually make anything happen, you won't deliver on your objectives.

From my experience, school leaders are very good at making things happen. The problem is, we have a tendency to take on too much ourselves and don't actually spend enough time on strategy and delivery through others. But that said, having worked with hundreds of school leaders, I do think there are some key things you can focus on. A number of these emerged from our G2G work in London. In particular we concluded that it was critical for leaders to focus on the recruitment of high quality staff, the retention of those who have the biggest impact and the removal of those who fail to make the grade.

In *Good to Great* Jim Collins (2001) uses the analogy of a bus to make this point. In this context, one of the most important things highly successful organisations do is get the right people on the bus, the wrong people off the bus, everyone in the right seats, and make sure the driver knows where the bus is headed. Of course, this particular analysis was originally based upon research in the business world and some heads have suggested that applying such principles in a school context is unrealistic, particularly as they perceive it is more difficult to tackle underperformance. Yet this is exactly what great schools do to create consistent delivery.

Topic 29

Consistency

Success isn't always about greatness. It's about consistency. Consistent hard work leads to success. Greatness will come.

Dwayne Johnson

Part of the *Good to Great* programme included working with Ann Berger, a former HMI. In one of the three presentations she made at the conferences, she outlined the key finding from an analysis of a number of Ofsted reports. Half of the reports were from schools that had achieved an overall effectiveness judgement of good and half were outstanding.

The most significant difference between the two sets of reports was that in the group of outstanding schools the word 'consistent' or 'consistently' was used far more often than in the good schools. In other words, schools on the journey to becoming great have recognised that it is important to not only have clarity around what should happen in school but have created an environment where this clarity translates into consistently applied practice.

To a large extent these schools are seeking to become high-reliability organisations. The commonly used analogy of the airline pilot is useful here. Our expectation as a passenger on a plane is that 100% of the journeys undertaken will be successful, with a safe take-off, flight and landing every single time. It is no good to us as passengers if the pilot's performance is only 95%; they need to get it right every single time.

In this topic, the example of creating a consistent climate for learning will be used to demonstrate some of the principles operating in the schools we studied.

There are a number of elements we have identified:

- Achieving buy-in and communicating effectively
- Using parents to support consistency
- Working with pupils
- Keep it simple, stupid (KISS)
- Responding to non-compliance
- A bedrock for creativity and innovation
- Building momentum

Achieving buy-in and communicating effectively

All successful schools long ago recognised the importance of achieving strong buy-in from their staff, pupils and parents. An important part of this process is to involve key stakeholders in the development of the policy. It is common for schools to involve their staff in a process of consultation when developing policies on a range of issues and managing behaviour should be no exception. However, many of the most successful schools have extended this consultation to include pupils and parents on the basis that the more people feel a sense of ownership of what is agreed, the more likely is the success of the policy.

The next crucial stage in gaining consistent application of these agreed processes and procedures is effectively communicating what has been set up. For staff this will probably involve the implementation of an effective training programme for all colleagues, not just teachers. This training should form an automatic and essential part of any new member of staff's induction programme. A simplified version is also often made available for visiting staff such as supply teachers, pupil teachers or even work experience pupils. There is also clearly explained documentation in schools' staff handbooks that outline how the systems and routines are expected to work.

Running alongside this, there is clear information made available to parents that explains how the schools' systems work. Many of these schools issue a handbook to parents when pupils start that covers all the key areas. The most effective schools will also make sure there is a direct and regular channel to update policies when they change.

It is also useful to remind parents of certain policies at those times of the year when they are particularly relevant. For example, for secondary schools, expectations relating to conduct, timekeeping and dress code for exams could be published just prior to the exam season beginning via the school's newsletter and website.

Using parents to support consistency

Parents who have relevant details about how different systems should be operated provide schools with a powerful tool in two respects. Firstly, when things go wrong, and a punishment is applied, parents may sometimes feel that their son or daughter has been unfairly treated. To be able to show parents that the school has simply implemented its agreed policies often leads to a shared agreement that the situation has been handled appropriately. The focus can then move on to how the school and parents can support the child in the future. It takes the emotion away from the decision. However, if the school hasn't followed its own procedures then the parents will have a legitimate concern.

Secondly, if parents know what should happen, they can spot when it hasn't. Staff know that they will be held accountable for their role in properly implementing systems. So long as parents feel able to raise concerns without school leaders becoming defensive, this feedback loop provides a powerful tool in maintaining consistency.

Working with pupils

The final group that need to be made aware of how the systems work is the pupil body itself. Schools need to make up their own minds about how much information to share with pupils directly. It could be argued that there should be a positive (if naïve) assumption that there aren't going to be any problems, and only explain the consequences of action as and when the need arises. In such a scenario, time would be spent in assemblies explaining the reward system to each year group with only basic reference to how the sanctions system will work.

This is often sufficient. When things do go wrong, pupils are very quick to notice how they are dealt with and will remember what action was taken, whether the misdemeanour was their own or that of a peer. What matters to them is that the system is followed fairly by the staff involved. If it is not, staff face the challenge of 'that's not fair' and the situation becomes even further from resolution. The desired response needs to be much nearer to 'fair cop, guv!'

The acknowledgement from those pupils who have done wrong and recognition that they have been treated fairly is an essential part of any restoration of relationships. Being treated more harshly than they know the system says they should gives a message that the member of staff has some reason to pick on them, thus making the way forward more challenging.

As with parents, it is important that pupils are able to discuss a situation where they have a genuine complaint about the application of procedures. The best school leaders will welcome this feedback as another mechanism for the promotion of consistency. It is not about giving in to pupils or taking sides, it is about being completely transparent about what is expected from all members of the school community.

Keep it simple, stupid (KISS)

For any set of policies to be consistently applied systems need to be simple. Overly bureaucratic systems that place unrealistic demands on staff will ultimately fail to pass this test as only a proportion of the staff will follow through agreed procedures. The most successful schools will have created procedures which they can confidently expect all staff to implement because everyone is able to see the benefits for them as individuals as well as for the school as a whole. They are a manageable set of arrangements that won't just be followed for a while, they will be followed by everyone for the long-term. Careful monitoring of such systems is therefore crucial in assessing whether they are working.

Responding to non-compliance

The very best schools, upon discovering inconsistent practice, will take one of two decisions. In certain cases, they will agree that action needs to be taken to deal with those individuals who either do not understand the procedures or appear unwilling to implement them for some reason. Clear decisive action here will also reinforce for others that this is important to the school and encourage them to continue to play their part in upholding expected standards. These schools recognise that every time an individual member of staff fails to follow agreed protocols, they make the job of maintaining high expectations and standards harder for everyone else. It is the consistent application of the agreed procedures that makes the difference.

Alternatively, if the reasons for procedures not being followed seem to suggest that the agreed procedures themselves are in some way in need of adjustment, a school may decide to review the policy itself. What the very best schools do not do is to simply carry on with the inconsistent application of procedures.

This only leads to a gradual deterioration of standards as more and more staff steadily stop following the agreed policy.

A bedrock for creativity and innovation

As explained earlier, this topic has only focused on one example of how schools strive to achieve consistency (in behaviour management) but these same principles can equally be applied to other areas of a school's work such as pedagogy, providing for continuing professional development or the provision of appropriate curriculum opportunities.

However, in general terms, this combination of clear purpose that is consistently applied is at the heart of our best schools. Contrary to some who fear this approach can stifle innovation, having consistently applied systems and procedures focused on specific goals does not hinder creativity. In fact, I would argue the opposite is true. Such a foundation provides the basis upon which schools can experiment, be creative and learn by making mistakes. They are able to grow and flourish, safe in the knowledge that the clarity around how things work at a basic level is secure.

In *Twelve outstanding secondary schools* Peter Matthews identified that consistency of approach was one of the key characteristics shared by all of the schools. 'They are truly corporate cultures, with staff and usually pupils working for each other sensitively and co-operatively. Pupils do not receive mixed messages or perceive staff to have vastly different values. They see common purpose: adults who are working in pupils' interests, who like being in the school, who care for it and are ambitious for its future.'

Building momentum

In *Good to Great*, Jim Collins describes what he calls the 'flywheel concept'. He asks the reader to consider how a typical flywheel works. Its principal aim is to store energy and build momentum. Pushing a heavy cast-iron disc is incredibly difficult in the early stages and progress appears slow. Gradually, over time, with a concerted and sustained effort the flywheel will build its momentum. As more and more people join in pushing the flywheel so its speed will grow and grow until eventually everyone could let go and the flywheel would continue unimpeded.

The analogy works in schools as well as in business. People instinctively want to join something that is building and growing. The fact that the departure of a key leader or other individuals does not mean the flywheel stops also effectively illustrates the importance of a whole organisation developing its own momentum rather than the alternative approach where the success of a school is dependent upon a single person or small group of people.

Reflecting on the leadership model that underpins this book, the flywheel analogy also reinforces the importance of alignment. If some people were pushing the flywheel in the opposite direction it would clearly not gain momentum. Everyone needs to be pushing in the same direction if success is to be achieved.

This idea of gradually building performance and delivery over time, with a focus on incremental improvement, underpins the concept of building *marginal gains*. This approach is exemplified by the success of the British cycling team which has concentrated on executing small changes really well. The combined impact of these changes has made them world class. The team believe that it is easier to make ten 1% improvements than it is to make one 10% change. This concept is, of course, at the heart of the incremental coaching approach outlined in Topic 30.

The role of staff development

What is clear about all highly successful organisations, whether they are schools or businesses, is the fact that they share a strong commitment to enabling all members of staff, at all levels of the organisation, to develop as professionals and thereby continually improve their performance.

However, as we listened to the stories of some of our most successful schools at G2G in London, it became clear that this process was far more than just a mechanical continuing professional development system linked to performance management and personal target setting. These schools had an organic sense of self-improvement fuelled by the genuine and self-motivated desire of all the individuals to make things better.

Jim Collins (2012) identified a key similarity in all the organisations he studied: a highly disciplined workforce. By this he didn't mean that there were strong command and control mechanisms operating. Rather, quite the reverse was true. Staff were highly focused around achieving their organisation's goals and were very self-motivated in trying to achieve them.

In our most successful schools the same is true. The staff strongly believe in acting in a collaborative way, reinforcing and emphasising a shared set of expectations and procedures. This self-discipline is not born of a fear of failing to follow the rules but arises out of a strong acceptance and understanding of the principles underpinning each school's success.

This notion is perhaps best illustrated by reference to an everyday challenge in many secondary schools: how to manage the behaviour of pupils in the corridor. The answer on one level appears very simple: it is the responsibility of all staff to both challenge unacceptable behaviour when they come across it as well as model appropriate behaviour. Of course, the reality is that in many schools some staff will and some staff won't respond appropriately. In our best schools, so strong is the shared sense of ownership of standards and expectations that no matter which member of staff comes across a pupil running in the corridor, one can be almost 100% certain that the matter will be dealt with appropriately.

Gaining such consistency of approach cannot be arrived at by monitoring or checking; nor is it usually the subject of a performance review target. It stems from a sense of pride and caring as part of a collaborative team dedicated and committed to a genuinely shared set of goals.

This sense of pride takes time to develop and is the result of a lot of hard work and resilience on the part of school leaders over a significant period of time.

Momentum brings resilience and strength in depth

There are times when schools encounter difficulties. In these circumstances the energy that the workforce as a whole is able to apply may diminish on a temporary basis. But where, as a leader, you have built strength in depth, where momentum and direction of travel has been clearly established, you are able to ride through temporary difficulty. The built up momentum carries you through. If, for example, a key member of staff leaves your team, such is the shared way of working and the clear understanding of 'the way you do things around here' that the team can absorb the temporary blip. No one is suggesting that maintaining high performance in schools is easy, but what does seem to help is strength in depth built up over a number of years.

The best schools, therefore, are the result of a relentless and focused effort sustained over time where all stakeholders are consistently pushing in the same direction; they represent an aligned implementation of policy where success breeds success and where it becomes hard for everyone in the school to resist joining in and becoming part of the story.

Key points
- How effective are you at getting buy-in?
- Are your systems and procedures designed to be as simple as possible?
- Does strong monitoring take place to make sure there is consistent application of policies?
- When consistency is not being achieved, do you investigate the situation and act accordingly?
- How much do you focus on staff development as a key element to achieving consistency?

Topic 30

Incremental coaching

I'm not asking any of you to make drastic changes to every single one of your recipes or to totally change the way you do business. But what I am asking is that you consider reformulating your menu in pragmatic and incremental ways to create healthier versions of the foods that we all love.

Michelle Obama

Learning in the workplace

When thinking about professional development in its widest sense, what has become strongly evident is that learning in the workplace is the most effective form of school improvement. And, of course, our best learning comes from when we make mistakes. It follows that the best schools will have encouraged a climate where risk taking and innovation are part of the everyday culture. Teachers and support staff in great schools are constantly trying new ideas and experimenting with the way they do things. This naturally leads them to reflect upon their own best practice which in turn leads to improved performance.

This can, of course, only happen in a school where making mistakes is seen as part of the process and not a reason to lay blame on someone. What was evident in hearing about best practice at many of the schools who have presented at our termly conferences has been how new ideas and innovation did not arise in their final form when they were first tried. Several iterations were often necessary before something was fit for purpose. Peter Matthews, in his Ofsted publication, found that not only do the best schools have a systematic and finely tuned system of planning performance management and professional development, they also link this with a culture of sharing best practice within each institution through regular coaching, mentoring and self-evaluation.

Setting aside quality time to reflect on performance and talk through challenges with someone who has good coaching skills can make a real difference. In the wider context, this approach is strongly validated by Daniel Goleman's work (2002) in which he recognises the short-term benefits of professional training, but advocates an approach based on ongoing workplace reflection and self-directed learning which he suggests has far greater long-term impact. In these circumstances staff take on their own learning agenda almost in spite of, rather than because of, traditional performance management processes. This is not to underestimate the crucial role such systems play. It's just that the highest performing institutions and schools are working at the next level where self-discipline and self-directed learning is at the heart of collective success.

1. The duration and rhythm of effective CPD support requires a longer-term focus. At least two terms to a year or longer is most effective, with follow up, consolidation and support activities built in.

2. Participants' needs should be carefully considered. This requires stepping away from a 'one size fits all' approach and creating content for teachers that integrates their day-to-day experiences and aspirations for their pupils with a shared and powerful sense of purpose.

3. Alignment of professional development processes, content and activities: ensuring there is a logical thread between the various components of the programme and creating opportunities for teacher learning that are consistent.

4. The content of effective professional development should consider both subject knowledge and subject-specific pedagogy in order to achieve the full potential of CPD, with clarity around learners' progress. In addition, content and activities should help teachers understand how pupils learn, both generally and in specific subject areas.

5. Effective professional development is associated with certain activities. These include explicit discussions, experimenting and testing ideas in the classroom and analysis of, and reflection around, the evidence and relevant assessment data.

6. External input from providers and specialists must challenge orthodoxies within a school and provide multiple, diverse perspectives. Facilitators acting as coaches and/or mentors should provide support through modelling, observation and feedback.

7. Empowering teachers through collaboration and peer learning: teachers should have opportunities to work together, try out and refine new approaches and tackle teaching and learning challenges.

8. Powerful leadership around professional development is pivotal in defining staff opportunities and embedding cultural change. School leaders should not leave the learning to teachers, they should be actively involved themselves.

Figure 44: What makes good CPD?

Adapted from a publication commissioned by the Teacher Development Trust from Durham University, Curee and UCL IoE (2015)

One school has weekly optional training for all staff and these sessions are very well attended. The staff leading the programme take suggestions on what to include and believe the high levels of attendance reflect the fact that what is on offer is tailored to what staff have said they are interested in. Rather than plan and publish in advance, the sessions are reactive and specific to immediate demand from staff. The topic will be announced each week, such as great group work, creating independence and positive relationship promotion.

As well as asking staff for suggestions, the senior team also identifies need and excellent practice while on daily learning walks and the staff themselves are encouraged to present at the weekly training sessions. In this way, all staff are given the opportunity to play a part in the development of others.

The role of incremental coaching

In the last few years I have become increasingly convinced that a powerful way to support teachers' development and improve the quality of teaching is to use regular 'incremental' coaching. I first came across this approach in Paul Bambrick-Santoyo's *Leverage Leadership* (2012).

His approach is based on avoiding some of the common errors he believes we make when thinking about how best to improve the performance of teachers. These are set out in Figure 45.

Error 1: More is better.

Top-tier Truth: *Less is more.* Many leaders fall prey to the temptation to deliver feedback on every aspect of the lesson. While that is a useful tool to demonstrate your instructional expertise, it won't change practice nearly as effectively. As we can learn from coaches in every field, bite-sized feedback on just one or two areas delivers the most effective improvement.

Error 2: Lengthy written evaluations drive change as effectively as any other form of feedback.

Top-tier Truth: *Face-to-face makes the difference.* The reason why this error persists nationwide among school leaders is that there is a subset of teachers for whom lengthy written evaluations are effective (just like there is a small group of learners for whom lengthy lectures are most effective). This leads to the dangerous conclusion that all teachers develop well by reading lengthy evaluations. In what other field do we subscribe to this idea?

Error 3: Just tell them; they'll get it.

Top-tier Truth: *If they don't do the thinking, they won't internalise what they learn.* In classroom instruction, highly effective teachers push the students to do the thinking. If teachers eclipse this thinking by providing conclusions or answers too quickly, students will disengage. Feedback is not any different: if teachers don't participate in the process of thinking about their teaching, they are less likely to internalise the feedback. This is metacognition applied to teacher development: having teachers think about their teaching improves their performance.

Error 4: State the concrete action step. Then the teacher will act.

Top-tier Truth: *Guided practice makes perfect.* If a surgeon simply tells a resident how to perform an operation, the resident will be less effective than if she practises with the surgeon's guidance. Teaching is the same: practising implementation of the feedback with the *leader* is at the heart of speeding up the improvement cycle. It also allows teachers to make mistakes before they're in front of the students again.

Error 5: Teachers can implement feedback at any time.

Top-tier Truth: *Nail down the timing.* Having a concrete timeline in which feedback will be implemented serves two purposes: it makes sure everyone has clear expectations as to when this will be accomplished and it will expose action steps that are not really able to be accomplished in a week.

Figure 45: Five errors to avoid when it comes to helping teachers improve
Adapted from *Leverage Leadership*, by Paul Bambrick-Santoyo (2012)

Incremental coaching adopts an approach that is designed to avoid these shortcomings. It typically involves a brief drop-in into a lesson followed by a short coaching conversation, ideally that day, which elicits the areas of strength and a single area of focus for improvement with some strategies to try. Ideally, the teacher has a chance to practise these as part of the follow-up conversation. The teacher then spends just one week really focusing on this single area for improvement until the next drop-in a week later when there can then be a discussion about the progress that has been made. This may result in another week or two on the same focus or the opportunity to move into a new area. As the model in Figure 46 suggests, the initial questioning is very open, allowing the teacher to work out as much as possible for themselves. Only if needed, are more closed or probing questions introduced. In all cases, clear actions for follow-up are clarified, with a clear timeline for each.

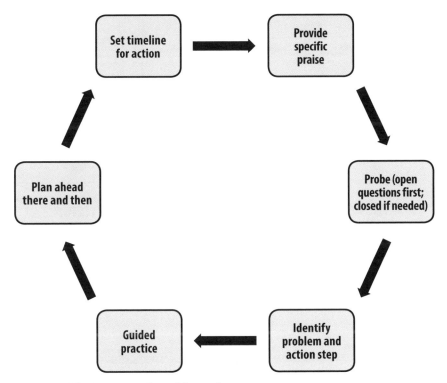

Figure 46: The incremental coaching cycle
Adapted from *Leverage Leadership*, by Paul Bambrick-Santoyo (2012)

Over time, this incremental process enables teachers to develop mastery in the full range of basic classroom skills and pedagogies that will lead to improved classroom delivery and improved outcomes for pupils. At its heart, the incremental coaching approach gives ownership for improvement to the teachers themselves.

At Torquay Academy, the incremental coaching cycle has been simplified somewhat. Figure 47 summarises their approach.

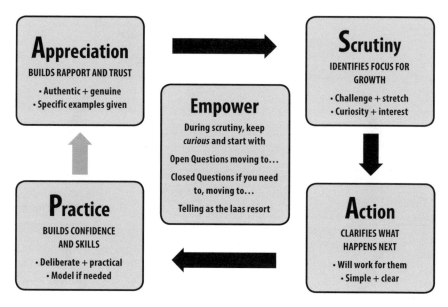

Figure 47: The ASAP model for incremental coaching
Torquay Academy

You will also see that as well as identifying the (reduced number of) stages in the process, the model also includes some of the processes and skills individuals need to adopt.

Matthews (2017) has looked into incremental coaching and believes its potential is significant: 'In the research carried out into incremental coaching I found that where it has been adopted by a school, incremental coaching is the core process for developing the teaching workforce; it builds on other training and is central to continuing professional development (CPD), effectively transforming continuing to *continuous* professional development. One further characteristic, essential to the successful establishment of incremental coaching, is that it is developmental and non-judgemental. It is best when detached from performance management; indeed, perceptions of such a link are detrimental to the process. For this reason it is better if coaches are not the line managers of those they are coaching, and the outcomes of coaching are owned by the coachee rather than management.'

Matthews also notes that the way in which incremental coaching is presented is crucial. The climate within which it is implemented makes a real difference: 'The schools presented incremental coaching as an entitlement for teachers: something that will support them in their work, enhance their skills and accelerate their progress towards professional mastery. Even when this stage is reached, it remains valuable, as demonstrated by leaders in education and other organisations and in a range of occupations. Coaching has the potential to make teaching more effective, more satisfying and more successful, through its agency for professional and personal growth. Undertaken systematically across a school, it can improve instructional quality and consistency.'

In other words, the approach is all about helping teachers be better teachers and is separated from the judgemental approach that sits behind formal lesson observations and appraisal. To refer back to an earlier topic, the focus is on 'fattening the pig, not weighing it'.

Figure 48 summarises Peter Matthews' description of the approach.

The term 'incremental coaching' encapsulates a *regular, frequent and ongoing cycle of observation and action-based coaching.* The coaching is a dialogue that typically includes review, praise, feedback, reflection, modelling, planning and goal setting. Essentially:

- The process focuses on one action step at a time.
- Each step is followed up in subsequent observations until it is demonstrably embedded in practice.
- There is a minimal interval between observation and coaching.
- The observation and coaching events are planned into the organisation of the school.
- Coaching is a disciplined activity which incorporates common elements.
- Coaches are trained in the process.
- Coaches are lead practitioners who have earned professional respect.

Figure 48: The ingredients of incremental coaching
Peter Matthews (2017)

From the feedback sandwich to feedback tennis
Much has been written about how to give great feedback to colleagues. When it comes to your leadership approach, I am increasingly of the view that the traditional feedback sandwich may have had its day!

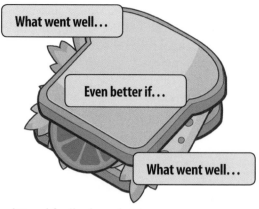

Figure 49: The traditional feedback sandwich

The idea behind the feedback sandwich is a good one. Make sure there is some positive stuff in among your feedback. In fact, make sure there is more positive than negative. And ensure there is something to improve or develop. All of which is great. The trouble with this approach is that individuals don't really own their area for growth, even though they may very well have their own ideas about how they can improve which are pretty similar. My response has been to apply the 'ask first' mantra outlined in Topic 38 to feedback, which has resulted in me coming up with a new approach that I am calling 'feedback tennis'!

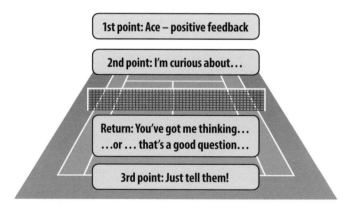

Figure 50: Feedback tennis

In feedback tennis, you still start off with some positives. These form your first point. Of course, these need to be authentic areas that you thought were genuinely good. You may also invite colleagues to come up with their own positive reflections. This approach can work whether it's reflecting on a lesson or on a something a leader has just delivered. By focusing on the positive, you are building rapport, trust and positivity.

Your **second point** is to ask a neutral or non-judgemental question about an area where you think there may be some potential for growth and see what your colleague thinks. There may be a very good reason why they did what they did that you weren't aware of. Or you may have contributed a question that has got them reflecting in a helpful way, genuinely open to thinking about ways they might improve what they did.

Such a response or **return** is what you are looking for. You have prompted colleagues to think for themselves. And of course, unlike the feedback sandwich that is eaten in just three bites, feedback tennis can continue back and forth as a coaching conversation until the point is made – or won!

There will, of course, be occasions when however well you ask curious questions, a colleague just can't see something for themselves. In such situations, it is absolutely appropriate for your **third point** to be that you tell them what you are thinking! They key here is to avoid falling into the trap of you making all the suggestions on the assumption that this is what your colleague needs. The more they have done the thinking for themselves, the greater the likelihood that their practice will change for the better and in the long term.

It's early days for feedback tennis as a concept (and my evidence for its efficacy is effectively zero) but informal feedback from colleagues who have focused on developing this as a leadership habit have said they are finding it very useful.

Key points

- What resonates with you about the concept of incremental coaching?
- Might the concept of feedback tennis be something you would like to explore in your context?
- If incremental coaching is something you want to explore, how will you plan its introduction carefully?

Topic 31

Appraisal meetings

The pessimist complains about the wind; the optimist expects it to change; the realist adjusts the sails.
William Arthur Ward

Although they are relatively rare events, it is worth just spending a moment to think about appraisal or performance management meetings and where they fit into the bigger picture of an individual's development. For many schools (and I was guilty of this!) appraisals run the risk of being a one-off event around the beginning or end of a school year. It has become increasingly evident to me that to be really effective formal appraisal meetings should be properly aligned with more regular developmental 1:1s that have a coaching focus. This is explored in more detail in Topic 28 on 1:1 meetings as well as in Topics 37–40 which look at the different elements of a coaching approach to leadership. Of course, you will need to flex the way this works to suit your context.

However, as Figure 51 summarises, there are some key features that make for really good appraisal meetings.

1. Agree time and place well in advance, **stick to these arrangements**, and be **well prepared** for the meeting.

2. Give the appraisee time to reflect on their goals and **rate themselves** in advance.

3. Ask them to also think about **areas for development** ahead of the meeting.

4. Wherever possible, give some **positive feedback** at the start.

5. Making sure you have **good evidence**, collected from a range of sources which has ideally been shared in advance.

6. There should be **no surprises**. If there are performance concerns, they should always be raised at the time they arise and support offered.

7. They should do more of the talking. **Ask good questions** to help them reflect for themselves on their strengths and areas for development.

8. Keep the meeting **appropriately formal**. It's not a social occasion and will usually matter a lot to the person being appraised. Take it seriously.

9. Take care in your write-up **not to over-praise or miss out concerns**. Both of these could come back to haunt you if performance dips.

10. Make sure new goals are **SMART** (specific, measurable, achievable, relevant and time-bound). Avoid setting goals that you both know will never be achieved.

11. Make sure you keep **good notes** and ask them to sign off (and comment, if they wish) on the final record of the meeting.

12. Ask for **feedback** on how you conducted the appraisal.

Figure 51: Twelve tips for great appraisal meetings

Key points

- How effective are your own appraisal meetings?
- What about across the organisation?
- Are there any quick wins you might consider implementing?

Difficult conversations

You're not learning anything unless you're having the difficult conversations.

Gwyneth Paltrow

Difficult conversations are one element of good accountability. Accountability isn't always perceived as a positive thing but in the long-term it really does make everyone's job easier and a school better. Schools with clear accountability structures, systems and cycles, with excellent quality assurance at every level, achieve great things. The structure has to be fair, mutually agreed, understood and consistent if it is to achieve optimum impact. Being held to account, when it is done well, should feel like a positive and rewarding experience. From the perspective of one of your teachers, for example, it is the feeling that you are clear about your role and responsibilities; you have been challenged by the requirements but have support in place if you need it. As you achieve benchmarks, you receive timely advice and constructive and helpful feedback and feel a sense of recognition and success when all has been achieved.

When accountability is used less wisely, it can create a fear factor in a school community or organisation. If people are less clear on their role or responsibility, they do not feel ownership and are quick to blame others or cover up mistakes rather than be honest. Accountability at its best is constantly demanding the highest performance from every individual in the organisation. People know what their role looks like if it is done outstandingly well. If standards are not met, leaders are unafraid to look the person in the eye and say: 'this is not good enough'. Swift intervention is undertaken and consequences enforced. How to approach these difficult conversations is described shortly in this topic.

Systematising your processes can be very helpful. You should try to be specific about what will be reviewed and when. You need to specify who will deliver the data or evidence required and outline the criteria for how its impact will be measured. You should aim to provide people with a checklist of what should be achieved in a typical week, month, term or year for each role in their team.

In the case of exam results, checking performance on a pupil-by-pupil basis is essential for good accountability. With this in place, how do you measure interim progress? What checks will you put in place to reassure yourself that you are on target and at which point should interventions, if necessary as a last resort, be put in place? A calendar and list of checkpoints should be shared with the success criteria clearly articulated, very similar to a mark scheme. This is a transparent and shared way of measuring success. At a whole-school level, there may be a rhythm to this already established.

Having difficult conversations

When it comes to tackling under-performance or inappropriate behaviour, there is a continuum, as shown in the diagram below. At one end of the spectrum are what I would call nudge conversations, where you gently raise an issue. Sometimes this is achieved through making light of a situation through humour or mentioning an issue in passing. In the majority of cases this can do the trick and the issue is resolved. By their very nature, these conversations are pretty easy to have. At the other end of the spectrum are those conversations that lead to someone leaving the school. While harder than nudge conversations, these are still relatively easy as things will have become untenable and by then the decision is clearly the right thing to do. Often the person may also not return to work, which again makes it a bit easier to manage.

Figure 52: The accountability continuum

The hardest conversations to have, the ones we tend to put off more than any others, are those that sit in the middle. You have tried nudging and it hasn't worked. At their worst, the outcome of these conversations is 'lose-lose'; you feel awful and the recipient feels destroyed. At best, the outcome is a 'win-win'; you feel as though you could not have delivered the message in a better way; and the recipient feels clear on their next actions and as though they have been treated in a fair way.

For a 'win-win' scenario, you need to think through what you want to say and the message that needs to be relayed. Practise it so that your words are clear, there is nothing worse than you thinking you have said it gently and them completely missing the point and carrying on with the behaviour! Make it short; the minute you carry on speaking, you muddle the message and talk yourself back out of it.

Putting off conversations you dread usually only makes them worse. But once you have had a few (conversations, not glasses of wine!), they do get easier. If you are about to have a difficult conversation, the work of Susan Scott (2003) who is well known for her work in this area, recommends covering the following in that start to the conversation, uninterrupted:

1. **N**ame the issue

2. Describe a specific **E**xample

3. Describe your **F**eelings about the issue

4. Clarify what is at stake, why this is **I**mportant

5. **A**ccept your contribution to this problem

6. Indicate your wish to **R**esolve the issue

7. Invite **T**hem to respond

The highlighted letters in this list can be an easy way for your middle leaders to remember the seven steps as they form the acronym **NEFI ART**. Critical in the process is making sure that once the situation has been set out you do not go on to try to solve the issue until you have an acceptance from the other person of the validity of the concern.

This all sounds fine in theory, but you need to ensure that you are properly prepared not only to give this introduction, but also for what may follow. There might be a whole range of responses from silence or anger, from complete denial to emotional collapse. Thinking through in advance how you might respond to each of these can be helpful.

You also need to try not to fall into the trap of 'propping up' the discussion that follows. Use questions to get the other person to talk and reflect on the issue, gain understanding and give a commitment to action. Let silences happen rather than be tempted to fill them. As Susan Scott suggests, let the silence do the heavy lifting. If the discussion goes off track, bring the dialogue back onto the issue you raised at the start.

You need to keep in mind your overall approach to managing the issue. Remember that in relation to Kilmann's 1994 model from Topic 23, in having a difficult conversation you are in forcing, collaborating or compromising mode. You are not smoothing or avoiding. This can be particularly important if you know you have a tendency to gloss over issues in the hope that they will go away or be tackled another time. You need to be disciplined. You also need to manage your own emotions, keeping to the facts at hand and the issue of concern.

If the conversation has gone well, the other person will not only have clarity about the issue, they will often feel relieved that it is out in the open and that a way forward has been agreed. You will usually go away feeling relived that you have done the hardest part, but do not forget the importance of monitoring the situation and offering support if needed.

Such discussions are serious, professional conversations. You cannot rely on or expect an existing friendship, personal loyalty or how long you have known and worked with someone to get you through such a meeting. On the other hand, you can't suddenly turn on 'seniority' mode and pull rank just to get your point across on a one-off occasion. Be empathetic, understanding and listen. Treat the recipient how you would wish to be treated if it were your line manager talking to you.

Allow the person to respond and, out of fairness, listen to what they say, but agree the issue and clear action points on what needs to happen. Finish with checking that they feel that they have been treated fairly. Where appropriate, clarify the action points in writing. It is important that the written part is supportive rather than seen as 'I am putting this in writing', which has different connotations. If the recipient feels that you have been fair, feels that what has been said is true, has a clear idea of how to respond and deliver and then does so, then you have had a 'win-win'.

After a difficult conversation

After a difficult conversation it can be tempting to pretend it didn't happen, particularly if the person works closely with you. It can sometimes just be a bit awkward. The best thing is to be proactive and take steps to keep dialogue open. Thank them for the conversation and focus on the agreed outcomes positively. Don't forget to make sure you hold them to account for what they have agreed to. Finally, you may wish to get involved in an activity with the person concerned that is nothing to do with what you have been discussing. Something you both enjoy. In a way, this approach isn't dissimilar from the *repair and rebuild* we might seek to undertake with a pupil!

Moving people on

For most staff, even when performance drops, a good conversation and some high quality support can get a situation back on track. But there will sometimes be times when you need to be clear about moving someone on when it is obvious they are not performing. All schools are required to have disciplinary and competency procedures, but in some they remain an underused vehicle for creating and maintaining high standards. There is nothing more frustrating for the hard-working and capable majority than to see a colleague who is not able or not interested in delivering to the desired standards being allowed to carry on unchallenged. Inevitably, if this situation is allowed to continue other colleagues may start to become demotivated and their own standards will quickly begin to drop.

Of course, all colleagues are entitled to an appropriate level of confidentiality in such situations, but the staff body as a whole is usually very quick to recognise when action has been taken to deal with the underperformance of a particular individual. This can be a powerful motivator among the wider staff who do see it as the role of leaders to ensure everyone on the team is delivering.

Over time, the culture in a school can change dramatically. As one of the outstanding schools I have worked with describes: 'we have become increasingly confident in supportively yet assertively setting clear expectations for underperforming colleagues. Without ever needing to publicise the fact, other colleagues recognise that this is happening and see it as a positive rather than a threatening aspect of our approach.'

How the very best schools go about addressing issues of underperformance varies from school to school and from case to case. In some schools where a culture of high expectations is well established, simply beginning a competency procedure with a member of staff can often be sufficient for them to take the decision to move on. The profession faces, however, a wider problem of how to prevent the recycling of such poor performers from one school to another, a debate that probably extends beyond the scope of this book.

In other scenarios, particularly where a member of staff may have particularly long service, schools often have a more informal conversation around the particular circumstances of that individual's career stage. Increasingly, this may involve reaching an agreed financial settlement.

Are you backing or sacking?

In all cases what all leaders should do is ensure that individuals that need it are offered 100% support in the first instance. Only if the required improvements fail to take place does it become necessary to consider the alternatives. This will involve working out an appropriate exit strategy and keeping to it.

The best schools have real clarity about where they are in the process and avoid vacillating between trying to support and trying to move someone on. When all else has failed, they take decisive action and relentlessly pursue the goal to move someone on. This 'backing or sacking' approach sounds somewhat draconian, but it is really important to be clear about where you are in tackling an individual's underperformance.

In schools where support is provided without clear targets and where a set period for performance review is not established, my own experience suggests this lack of clarity can lead to a failure to take decisive action to remedy the situation. Underperformance can go on for long periods where a school recognises the problem but almost unconsciously accepts it. Our pupils deserve better than this. They only have one chance.

Key points

- How good are you and your colleagues at having difficult conversations? What is the cultural norm?
- Might NEFI ART be a useful way to prepare and execute these conversations?
- Are you clear about whether you are backing or sacking at any given point in time when a colleague's performance is causing concern?

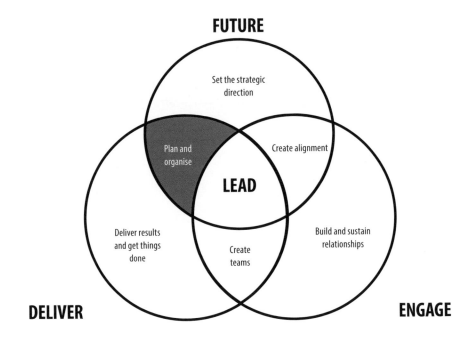

FUTURE

Set the strategic
direction

Plan and
organise

Create alignment

LEAD

Deliver results
and get things
done

Create
teams

Build and sustain
relationships

DELIVER

ENGAGE

Plan and organise

People don't resist change. They resist being changed.
Peter Senge

At its heart, the role of any leader is all about making change happen, not just for a while but for the long term. Whether that be improving the performance of a colleague in a particular area of practice, or designing and implementing a new policy or curriculum, the key to the success of any change is that it sticks. Too often in schools someone focuses on improving an area of practice, but not for long enough or in a sufficiently systematic way to ensure a change is embedded and will have a long-term impact on pupil outcomes.

Similarly, when it comes to developing a new policy or approach, an individual can sometimes introduce a new idea without properly engaging with those who will be responsible for making it happen or really thinking through how it will be implemented in practice. Before long the idea has withered on the vine or, at best, is being inconsistently applied.

Topic 33

Prioritisation

What may be done at any time
will be done at no time.
Scottish proverb

If there's one thing all school leaders have in common, it's the fact that it just seems like there's never enough time to do the job. Apart from managing the workload associated with your classes, including preparation and marking, there's everything you are accountable for in your leadership role. But have you ever stopped and really thought about what you do with your time, or think about whether there are things you could do to ease the burden and make things more efficient? And don't forget this doesn't just apply to you. It applies to all your staff, whatever your role. Ensuring staff have manageable workloads is a key action leaders need to take in building discretionary effort and increasing retention rates.

Approaches to managing time

The reality is that people have very different approaches to the use of time. Some people are actually energised by deadlines and find it most productive to work right up to them. Others can't bear the thought of having everything left until the last minute and will want everything planned out well in advance. Then there are those who just can't say 'no' when a job comes up. These are people who never stop to ask themselves whether they have time to do everything they have agreed to. Others are great procrastinators who will always find something else to do other than the things they really should be doing. Finally, there are those who just have to spend the time to get the detail right, even if that means other things are delayed or stress levels rise.

You probably know leaders that fit all of these descriptions. You may also find it interesting to reflect on your own predispositions in this respect! For all leaders, when it comes to better time management, knowing your own predispositions can be helpful.

So what can you actually do to manage your time more effectively? To start with, if you resolve to make the time, you may want to log how you spend your time over the course of a typical week. This will give you an idea about how much time you spend in each of the three circles in the leadership model shown in Figure 53. Typically, experience tells me school leaders find their time being sucked into the 'Deliver' circle, with insufficient time devoted to the equally important areas of 'Future' and 'Engage'.

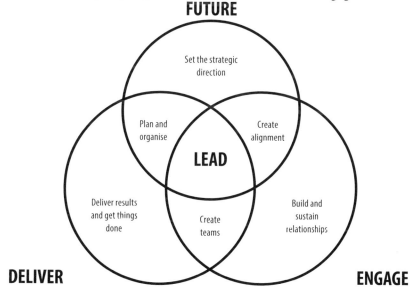

Figure 53: Six key areas for leadership action
Adapted from David Pendleton's Primary Colours model and Steve Radcliffe's Future – Engage – Deliver

You may also want to reflect on the Pareto Principle as shown in Figure 54. Basically, what Pareto helpfully reminds us is that typically we can achieve 80% of a result from 20% of effort. To achieve the same task perfectly takes a disproportionately larger amount of time (the remaining 80%). Just consider for a moment, the difference in taking on five tasks and giving them 20% effort (thus achieving a result of 400%) versus just doing one thing perfectly (resulting in a 100% result). One is clearly far more efficient.

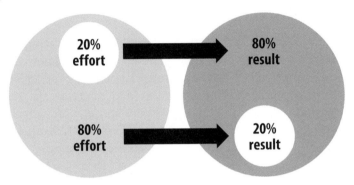

Figure 54: The Pareto Principle
Koch (1998)

While this clearly won't translate exactly to every goal we have in school, there is something worth reflecting on here. If you have the habit of wanting everything to be perfect, you may actually be being less efficient than you could be. Of course, there are some things that need to be 100% right. I am not suggesting getting the books to only *roughly* balance, for example! But I do think there is something we can learn from this approach.

Practical action

There are some simple practical things that can help you and your team. You probably do many of these already, but how ruthless are you in carrying them out? It is precisely when the pressure starts to build that most people tend to throw logic and reason out of the window and just respond to things as they arrive on their desk.

Goal setting

Set yourself goals. These are not the same as to-do lists. They are strategic things you and your team want to achieve in a given time frame. They should drive your overall planning. Break the goals down into small manageable chunks. You need to be realistic when setting your goals. There is nothing more satisfying than meeting a goal and nothing more frustrating than always failing to achieve them.

Just say no

If you are one of those people who just can't say 'no' then learn to. You will be surprised how quickly people will find someone else to ask!

Schedule time for the important but not urgent

It can be helpful to plan out when you are going to get certain things done. Not only does this help with the temptation to put things off, it means you can let others know what you are doing. This can be important if you find too much of your time is dealing with 'incidents' that maybe others can help with on a rota basis. It will also help reduce interruptions, particularly if you combine this with something as simple as saying to your team that if your door is closed, you would prefer not to be interrupted.

Avoid procrastination; eat your frog!

If you are prone to putting things off, you need to develop ways that help you get down to business. Often, the hardest part is just getting started. There is a school of thought that says you should try to make the very first thing you do each day the thing you are least looking forward to doing. The idea is that you immediately feel pleased once this task is done and are consequently much more efficient and energised than you would be if the job you are dreading were still hanging over you. Try it. It really works! You can also search for 'Eat the Frog' on YouTube to see a short video on this.

Set time limits

If you are prone to just working until the job gets done, you can be sure you will have absolutely no work-life balance. If this is your tendency, set yourself strict time limits and make sure you stick to them. If that means something will have to wait until tomorrow, then so be it.

Delegate more

This is easy to say and hard to do but there are lots of ideas in Topic 26. How often do you ask yourself if someone else could do a particular task? If you do, how often do you decide not to ask someone to do something because you think:

- others are just as busy as you are
- they aren't paid to do this
- they won't do it as well or as quickly as you will
- someone might think you are shirking your responsibilities?

All these reactions are typical and sometimes true. But often people make all kinds of assumptions about what others are thinking or are prepared to do. You will be surprised how carefully chosen tasks, planned in advance, can be seen by others as a great opportunity to develop as well as make an important contribution to the team. The key is not to do this in a way that feels like you are just dumping a problem on someone else at the last minute because you can't be bothered to do it or haven't planned properly.

A model for prioritisation

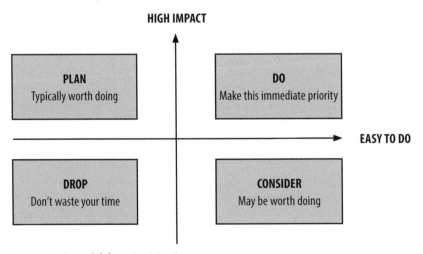

Figure 55: A model for prioritisation

Do

These are your classic win-wins. Easy to do and have a big impact: why wouldn't you do them?

Drop

These are the things that are hard to do and make little difference: why on earth are you still doing these? The answer is sometimes because someone else has asked you to! Time to have a *managing up* conversation – see Topic 19.

Plan

These are things which will make a big difference but are hard to do. A good strategy is to plan ahead, breaking the task into more manageable chunks and celebrating at each step of the way. These tasks also require you block out larger chunks of time and do all you can to protect this time.

Consider

These are easy-to-do tasks, but they don't make that much difference. You might want to do some of them, after all ticking off a few things on the to-do list is good for the soul! When I was a teacher I would spend 20 minutes at the end of a day on a Friday fiddling with my displays. It wasn't going to transform my teaching, but it did help create a welcoming environment for pupils and I found it a very therapeutic end to my week. The key here is not doing jobs in this box at the expense of those in the hard to do but high impact top left box.

So effective time management is all about being pro-active in the way you use this precious commodity. Don't allow yourself to be the victim of your circumstances or your own predispositions. Take control and discover how much more is possible when you set yourself some simple but important goals to achieve.

MICK reviews

One school I have worked with uses a very simple tool to review with staff how they could be more effective when it comes to time. Every half-term they give all staff the chance to contribute to a MICK review. Figure 56 sets out what's involved.

More	What is working well that we should do more of?
Include	What would help us achieve our goals that we don't currently do?
Change	What do we do that is important but not quite working at the moment?
Kick-out	What do we do at the moment that we could probably manage without?

Figure 56: carrying out a MICK review

What is powerful about this model is that it allows staff a voice to feed back to more senior staff about what might be in the *Drop* box as well as encouraging innovation and recognition of what is important to keep doing or improve.

Potential areas for review

Figure 57 sets out some areas where you may want to take a good hard look at what you do and decide where on the ease-versus-impact grid your current practice sits.

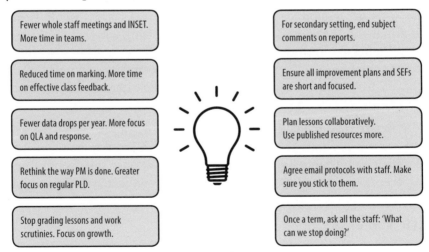

Fewer whole staff meetings and INSET. More time in teams.

For secondary setting, end subject comments on reports.

Reduced time on marking. More time on effective class feedback.

Ensure all improvement plans and SEFs are short and focused.

Fewer data drops per year. More focus on QLA and response.

Plan lessons collaboratively. Use published resources more.

Rethink the way PM is done. Greater focus on regular PLD.

Agree email protocols with staff. Make sure you stick to them.

Stop grading lessons and work scrutinies. Focus on growth.

Once a term, ask all the staff: 'What can we stop doing?'

Figure 57: Potential areas to reduce workload
Adapted from a blog by Sherrington (2017)

Key points

- Does the Pareto principle resonate in your context?
- Might 'eating the frog' help you or colleagues?
- Could the prioritisation grid be useful in identifying how you could be more effective?
- Could the MICK review idea be useful in your context?
- Is there anything in Figure 57 that looked at potential areas where workload might be reduced that could be a quick win for you?

Topic 34

Managing change

Change will not come if we wait for
some other person or some other time.
We are the ones we've been waiting
for. We are the change that we seek

Barack Obama

So how do you approach changing things in a way that will bring
about sustainable impact for your pupils? There are numerous theories
about how to 'do' change. Many originate with leadership and change
management guru John Kotter. A professor at Harvard Business School
and world-renowned change expert, Kotter introduced his eight-step
change process in his book *Leading Change* in 1996.

Figure 58: Eight steps of change
John Kotter (1996)

Step one: increase urgency

For change to happen, it helps if the whole team or the school really wants it. So how do you engage staff when there is a natural resistance to change? How do you develop a sense of urgency around the need for change? It isn't simply a matter of you showing staff a set of plateauing test results or scaring them about Ofsted, the demands of a new curriculum or an attendance target. It is about you instigating an open, honest and convincing dialogue about what's happening in the educational landscape and with your context. You might decide it would be useful to identify potential problems that lie ahead if they don't change, and develop scenarios showing what could happen in the future. However you achieve this, you need to start honest discussions and give dynamic and convincing reasons to get people talking and thinking.

Step two: build a 'change-team'

As with any whole-school change, if time permits it's a good idea to get a small group of people to work up your ideas. Using your change-team to help develop your plans is useful in itself. But having them as a small group of advocates for the rest of the team can be very powerful, particularly if you have managed to include one or two key influencers in your group.

If you are leading across more than one school, steps one and two in Kotter's model are particularly important if you are going to gain the traction you are likely to need.

Step three: get the vision right

When you first start thinking about change, there will probably be many great ideas and solutions floating around. You need to link these concepts to an overall vision that people can grasp easily and remember. A clear vision can help everyone understand why you're asking them to do something. When people see for themselves what you're trying to achieve, then the directives they're given tend to make more sense. Consulting on the vision for a change can also be a good way for you to help generate interest in making it work.

Step four: communication for buy-in

What you and your change-team do with your plans after they have been created is crucial. Your message will probably have strong competition from other day-to-day pressures and priorities, so you need to communicate it frequently and powerfully, and embed it within everything that you do. You need to keep telling the story.

Involving pupils and parents in this stage can be a powerful way of building buy-in for an idea. It also helps the staff see the benefits for the pupils in a way they may not have quite appreciated.

It's also important for you, as the driver of the change to 'walk the talk'. What you actually do is often far more important – and believable – than what you say. You should demonstrate the kind of behaviour that you want from others.

Step five: enable action

If you follow these steps and reach this point in the change process, you've been talking about the vision and building buy-in. Hopefully, staff want to get busy and achieve the benefits that you have been promoting.

But is anyone resisting the change? And are there processes or structures that are getting in its way? There is further guidance towards the end of this topic about how you might approach this.

It's also important for you to identify and put in place the structure for change, and continually check for barriers to it. Removing obstacles can empower the people you need to execute the vision, and it can help the change move forward. One way to do this is to delegate to mini-teams. A great example here is on curriculum planning. Pairing up members of your team to devise a unit of work, where the pairings have been carefully thought through, can be a great way to remove obstacles to engagement in change. At a more senior level, using sub-teams to deliver on a change can be a great way of playing to strengths and keeping things manageable.

Step six: create short-term wins

Nothing motivates more than success. Look out for ways you can give your staff a taste of victory early in the change process. This could be a month or a year, depending on the type of change, but they'll want to have results they can see. Without this, critics and negative thinkers might impact on your progress. People need to quickly be thinking that the change is a good thing – they need to 'feel the benefit' fast.

Step seven: don't let up

Kotter argues that many change projects fail because victory is declared too early. Real change runs deep. Quick wins are only the beginning of what needs to be done to achieve long-term change. In particular you need to tackle those that don't appear to be on board with the change. Typically, these 'laggards' are the last to adopt any change. If you have spent time properly defining how the change will work at stages two and three, then these are easy conversations to have. There is nothing worse than saying to someone that they need to make a change when you know deep down it isn't 100% the right thing to be doing.

Each success you have also provides an opportunity to build on what went right and identify what can be improved. Make sure they take time to reflect, as a team, on 'what went well' and 'even better if'.

Step eight: make it stick

Finally, to make any change stick, it should become part of your culture. It should be consistently applied. A team's culture often determines what gets done, so the values behind the vision must show in day-to-day work.

Your systems for monitoring need to place a value on the things you have changed to help embed them. The key milestones should be part of the wider team or school's development plan. How you recognise and celebrate success, both as a school and as a team, also needs to reflect the changes you have made.

Enabling action

Stage five of Kotter's model is about making sure there is nothing to stop a change being successful; it's about making sure that all the key ingredients for a successful change are in place. This is where Kotter's model overlaps usefully with another change model from Knoster, Thousand and Villa (2000) set out in Figure 59.

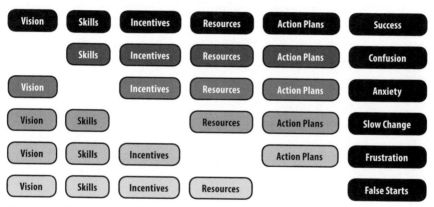

Figure 59: Dimensions of change
Knoster, Thousand and Villa (2000)

As the model suggests, if one key element is missing it will have consequences. At the back of the Leadership Matters Journal there are a series of blank checklists for change which are a useful summary of both key models. There is more on using checklists in Topic 35.

The LM Template section of the Leadership Matters website also has a Word version of the checklist for change document.

Managing the effect of change on others

People respond differently to change. But all of us, when there is a major change happening, tend to go through a series of stages of how we feel about the change. This can also affect our own feelings of self-worth or competence. It is not uncommon for people to doubt they can perform successfully in the way a change may demand. The most commonly known model for illustrating how this happens was developed by Elisabeth Kübler-Ross (1969) and is shown in Figure 60.

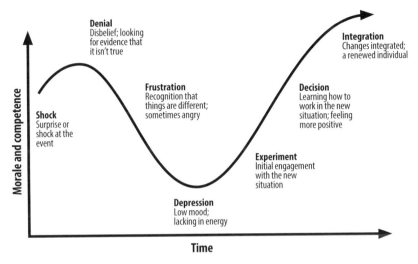

Figure 60: The change curve
Adapted from the Kübler-Ross model

When you are introducing a significant change, it is well worth taking some time out to think about how each of the individuals in the team are likely to react and then work out the best way to approach things with them, without compromising on your overall goals. As a school, you may wish to use one of the personality predisposition tools available, such as those we have developed at Leadership Matters, to support this. Once again, this is about understanding your situation before acting.

In addition to using Kotter's eight-step model as a useful guide to thinking about change and thinking about how different team members may respond to change, you may also want to consider these points:

1. Keep the change you want to make as simple as possible. This makes it easier to communicate, easier to get buy-in, easier to deliver consistently and easier to monitor impact.

2. When you consult on a particular change, you should remember to thank everyone who has taken the time to give you feedback and welcome their input, even though some of it may be negative. Giving people a proper chance to get things 'off their chest' can be an important part of the change process.

3. After consultation, always make sure you feed back what you have heard. In particular where you have decided not to act on a particular viewpoint, you should take the time to explain why. This is often best done face-to-face. It is important for people to feel they have been heard, even if, in the end, their argument hasn't won the day (from my experience, school leaders aren't good at this).

4. You should be prepared to be flexible, but only if in doing so you can take more people with you and still make the change you want to make. Showing flexibility can also be important if the change you have made doesn't appear to have been successful. If, after a sufficient period of time, there is clear evidence that the whole team has worked hard for a change, but it isn't delivering the impact you had hoped, it is a sign of strength to acknowledge this and find another way forward.

Using your resources wisely to deliver

There are never enough resources to do everything you would like to do. Budgets are always tight. Whether we are working in the public or private sector, there is a responsibility on all of us in education to make sure we are spending our limited resources to their best effect. This requires proper planning. It is also important for all leaders to ensure financial probity. Systems need to be in place to ensure that the purchasing of goods and services is carried out through due financial process and that any income generation is handled appropriately.

The resource planning cycle

At its simplest level, there are four key stages to the process of strategic resource planning. These can equally be applied to leaders at all levels:

1. Agreeing your overall strategic *aims*, including any new strategic priorities you wish to undertake.

2. Agreeing your strategic *plan*. This sets out how you plan to achieve your aims.

3. Working out the *cost* of the different elements of your strategic plan. This will include working out any on-going running costs that need to be covered as well as any start-up costs that may relate to new initiatives that you want to implement.

4. Ensuring you are getting the best *value* for money for your investment. This will require thinking carefully about how you procure goods or services as well as how you ensure you make efficient use of the resources at your disposal. More on this later.

There is a whole other language around resource management, some of which sounds far more complex than it actually is. You may well know what many of the terms below mean but just in case, here are a few definitions you might find helpful as reminders.

Revenue and capital costs
Revenue costs are recurring costs, year on year. They include items like staffing, consumables and on-going replacement for items such as furniture. Capital expenditure is one-off spending on items that won't need replacing for some time, such as a new suite of computers or a new classroom.

Economy
This refers to keeping costs as low as possible. It is about getting a good price for the items or services you are purchasing. Typically, researching the market and buying in bulk helps drive down costs and improve economy.

Efficiency
This refers to how you use what you have procured. You may have purchased a new microscope at a great price, but if it is hardly ever used, that is a very inefficient use of the resource. Likewise, expenditure on IT equipment and software that is used by the whole team, the whole time, is a very efficient use of resource.

Effectiveness
This relates to whether your spending gives good value for money. It isn't simply about how cheap something was to purchase or how well it is being used. It is the overall judgement about the impact of your spending in

relation to what you are trying to achieve. Measuring effectiveness is much more difficult than measuring economy or efficiency, but it is ultimately the most important judgement to make. It is an old cliché, but the cheapest isn't always the best. What matters is delivering great value for money.

There has been a lot of research undertaken in recent years about the relative effectiveness of the different ways schools spend their money. Figure 61 sets out some of the key messages emerging from this research. Again, this is probably something you are already familiar with but is included here for completeness.

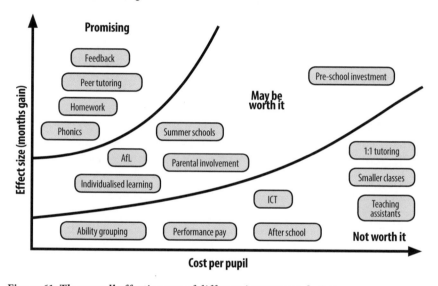

Figure 61: The overall effectiveness of different investment decisions

Adapted from the Education Endowment Foundation Teaching and Learning Toolkit (2013)

You might be surprised to see the impact of smaller class sizes and the typical effectiveness of the use of teaching assistants or the use of 1:1 tuition. Of course, this research is based on the typical impact of these different approaches rather than what is the case in individual schools, but it gives us all serious food for thought.

As with all evidence, the important thing is to consider it within your context. As Dylan Wiliam says, 'What works is not the right question.

Everything works somewhere. Nothing works everywhere. What's interesting is *under what conditions* does this work?' The most recent research from the Education Endowment Foundation (2015) on the effective use of teaching assistants is a case in point. The overall analysis for the impact of using TAs in the way they tend to be used suggests they represent poor value for money, but when used in the right way they can have significant impact. Figure 62 summarises the key findings of this research.

1. TAs should not be used as an informal teaching resource for low-attaining pupils.
2. Use TAs to add value to what teachers do, not replace them.
3. Use TAs to help pupils develop independent learning skills and manage their own learning.
4. Ensure TAs are fully prepared for their role in the classroom.
5. Use TAs to deliver high quality one-to-one and small group support using structured interventions.
6. Adopt evidence-based interventions to support TAs in their small group and one-to-one instruction.
7. Ensure explicit connections are made between learning from everyday classroom teaching and structured interventions.

Figure 62: Making the most of teaching assistants – key recommendations
Education Endowment Foundation (2015)

Key points

- Do you and colleagues use any models to help you plan change?
- Might using or creating a checklist for change be useful?
- How good are you and colleagues at looking at what the evidence suggests?
- Could you plan and budget even more effectively?

Topic 35

Checklists

Under conditions of complexity,
not only are checklists a help, they
are required for success.
Atul Gawande

When pilots prepare to take-off and land they always use a checklist to make sure they do what they need to do, and do it in the right order. Even in the high-tech world of aviation, the simple paper checklist still has its place. I suspect schools are no different.

Checklists can be useful in all sorts of contexts, from planning and delivering a successful parents' evening to ensuring pupils make an effective transition from one key stage to another. Once created, colleagues can share checklists easily rather than re-invent the wheel each time that something needs doing. It's a great way to build and refine a school's culture and capture its institutional memory.

As an example, Figure 63 shows what a checklist for managing change might look like. Based on some of the change models already mentioned in Topic 34, it can help busy school leaders make sure they don't miss out critical parts of the change process that can, in certain situations, scupper a whole initiative.

Action	When	Notes
Be clear why change needed – get people wanting change		
Get a small group working on it and review the evidence of what works		
Create a draft vision and proposal		
Test it out with people		
Make sure everything is in place (especially skills and time to do it)		
Launch		
Ensure quick wins		
Get real-time feedback		
Challenge those not adopting		
Build into standard routines for planning and evaluation		

Figure 63: An example of a checklist for change

Topic 29 was all about how we can create consistency of effective practice. It doesn't mean everyone does everything the same, but it does mean there are simple systems and processes in place that ensure delivery is reliable, and checklists can be a useful way to achieve this. If you want to read more on checklist methodology and impact, some great work has been published by Atul Gawande in *The Checklist Manifesto* (2011).

Key points

- Could using checklists more often help you or a colleague be more reliably effective?
- How might you build this idea into your culture?

Topic 36

Personal organisation

He who would do good to another must do it in minute particulars; general good is the plea of the scoundrel, hypocrite and flatterer: for art and science cannot exist but in minutely organized particulars.

William Blake

Your personal organisation can make a big difference to your own effectiveness as a leader as well as the levels of motivation or discretionary effort of those you work with. Get this right and the culture and climate within your team or organisation will significantly improve.

In Topic 22 we examined the importance of those day-to-day actions where we can sometimes slip up. As a recap, here are some of the key things we identified people find frustrating, such as leaders who:

- don't reply to a letter or e-mail within a day or two of it being sent
- regularly turn up late to teach or to meetings because they have been dealing with 'more important' matters
- leave colleagues out of the loop regarding a particular issue or event

- forget to do things that they said they would do or even do something differently from that which had been previously agreed
- ask for feedback at the end of event and then fail to act upon it or even acknowledge the feedback the next time the event is organised
- don't meet deadlines that all staff are expected to meet
- make (often poor) decisions 'on the hoof' because they have failed to plan ahead effectively.

Keeping commitments

One of the most frustrating things for members of staff in any school is when someone senior doesn't keep a promise they made. It is probably the quickest way that trust can be destroyed. Yet honouring commitments, especially when it is clearly difficult to do so, is also one of the most effective ways you can build confidence and trust with staff, pupils and parents.

Leaders can often be tempted to wriggle out of commitments that they may have made. Often this will arise in situations where a promise is given before thinking through all its implications.

For example, a head that agrees, as a result of some special pleading, that a particular member of staff may have a reduced timetabled commitment. They may well find themselves in the position where other staff complain this is unfair. The temptation, of course, is to renege on the promise made. Yet it is probably wiser to honour the original agreement and openly apologise to the other colleagues that an error had been made which would be rectified in future. The ability to say sorry and acknowledge the error is critical here. Trying to make excuses and blame changing circumstances can be tempting but reduces trust.

This example also serves to illustrate the importance of carefully thinking through commitments and promises before making them.

Don't drop the ball

What systems do you have in place to make sure things you have decided, agreed or promised to do, actually get done? For some leaders, this is all about lists. Some of you will be naturally very organised and for you what follows may not be of interest or much use. But a surprising number of school leaders are not that predisposed to being well organised. The great news is, there are a number of simple and effective ways you can keep organised. One way is to use your email account to help. Many school leaders I have worked with over the last few years have found this technique has really helped them. Here's how this system, which I still use to this day myself, actually works.

Stage one: a job arrives
A particular task may arrive through different routes. Some may arise, for example from a meeting, a conversation in the corridor or an email. Others may be things you decide for yourself you want to do. However your jobs arrive, what I find useful is having just one place where you store them.

Stage two: creating one place for your job list
For those tasks that don't arrive by email, one should ideally have one place (a notebook or diary) where jobs are written down. It may sound like a small point but bear with me because this next strategy really works! Next to your notes, where there is a task, draw a large circle. This serves to indicate that action is needed and will really stand out on the page.

When it comes to reviewing the empty circles – something you should ideally do at least once a day – you have two options: either do the job straight away and tick the circle, or send yourself an email with the task written in the email header.

This means that you then have all your outstanding tasks in your email system. Given that many tasks actually arrive by email these days, this stage is often unnecessary, which is why this is so efficient as a methodology for managing jobs.

Stage three: managing your email
There is nothing worse for many school leaders than an overflowing inbox. It adds to that sense of feeling overloaded and overwhelmed. I have worked with school leaders at all levels in the last few years and some of them have literally thousands of emails in their inbox. There has to be a better way!

My suggestion is this: create just three email folders labelled *Now*, *Soon* and *Later*. You can then place emails into the appropriate box, (not forgetting the option to press delete!) thus keeping your inbox clear.

You may of course want to vary how many folders you have or what you call them. You also may want to create other folders to archive emails that you might want to find later, although I would actually suggest this isn't a great use of time. Much better to just store any email you think you may need again in your system's archive folder and use the search engine within your email account on the rare occasion you need to retrieve a particular email.

The advantage of this system is that all your jobs are now in one place. Re-prioritising is easy, you just move emails between the folders. Schedule a short amount of time each day to review your *Now* and *Soon* boxes. You only need to review the *Later* box once a week to see if anything can be deleted (many can) or moved into Now or Soon because the time has come to action them.

This method has other benefits. When you are in a meeting or talking in a corridor and you have agreed to help out with something, why not just ask the other person to email you as a reminder. That serves two purposes: it means they have to make the effort to do this which means they really need your help, and you automatically have it in your tasks system, rather than having to transfer it from your notebook or that scrap of paper you wrote it on and lost. This of course assumes you wrote something down at all! Many heads I know think they are great at remembering to do things. They usually aren't – there are just too many things on that mental 'to do' list.

Using this simple email-based prioritisation system has transformed may leaders' personal effectiveness and their ability to prioritise efficiently. You may not need something like this, but if you are struggling with the sheer volume of tasks and worry that you may be dropping balls without even realising it, why not give it a try!

Key points

- How good is your own personal effectiveness?
- How do you know? Don't forget LM 360 is one way to get feedback on this.
- Might adopting the email-based task and prioritisation system be useful in your context?

Section D

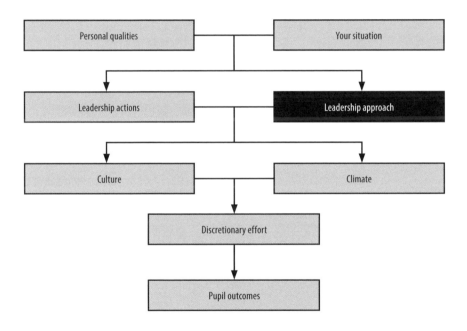

Leadership approach

One of the best paradoxes of leadership
is a leader's need to be both stubborn
and open-minded. A leader must insist
on sticking to the vision and stay on
course to the destination. But he must
be open-minded during the process.
Simon Sinek

The previous part of this book focused on the key areas that school leaders need to take action on:

- Defining the vision and strategic approach
- Creating alignment
- Building and sustaining relationships
- Creating teams
- Planning and organising
- Delivering results and getting things done

This part will explore not the *what* but the *how*: your leadership approach. The first topic will focus on leadership style. The remaining three topics will look at the habit of *asking first*, a coaching approach and the GROWTH coaching model.

Topic 37

Leadership styles

It ain't what you do; it's the way that you do it.
Melvin Oliver and James Young

So what do we mean by leadership style? Why does leadership style matter? Are some leadership styles more effective than others? Daniel Goleman, who is probably best known for his work on emotional intelligence, has also investigated the impact of leadership style on the climate of organisations.

In his 2000 paper *Leadership that gets results* he identified that, as leaders, we tend to use the following six different leadership styles:

Visionary (authoritative)
Primary objective: providing long-term direction and vision. You tend to:

- develop and articulate a clear vision
- solicit staff perspective on the vision and see selling the vision as key to success
- persuade staff by explaining the rationale for the team's best long-term interests

- set standards and monitor performance in relation to the wider vision
- motivate with a balance of positive and negative feedback.

Affiliative

Primary objective: creating staff harmony. You tend to:

- be concerned with promoting friendly interactions
- place more emphasis on addressing staff needs than on goals and standards
- pay attention to, and care for, the whole person; stress things that keep people happy
- avoid performance related confrontations
- reward personal characteristics more than job performance.

Directive (coercive)

Primary objective: compliance. You tend to:

- give lots of directives, not direction
- expect immediate staff compliance
- control tightly
- rely on negative, corrective feedback
- motivate by imposing sanctions for non-compliance, with few rewards
- rarely explains rationale, only negative consequences.

Democratic

Primary objective: building commitment and generating new ideas. You tend to:

- trust that staff can develop the appropriate direction for themselves and the school
- invite staff to participate in decisions
- reach decisions by consensus
- delegate decision-making as well as tasks

- hold many meetings and listen to staff concerns
- reward adequate performance; rarely give negative feedback.

Pacesetting

Primary objective: making rapid progress and achieving tasks to high standards of excellence. You tend to:

- lead by example and have high standards: 'look at me; do what I am doing; keep up with me'
- expect others to know the rationale behind what is being modelled
- are apprehensive about delegating
- take responsibility away if high performance is not forthcoming, and have little sympathy for poor performance
- rescue the situation or give detailed task instructions when staff experience difficulties.

Coaching

Primary objective: long term professional development of others. You tend to:

- help staff identify their unique strengths and weaknesses
- encourage staff to establish long-range development goals
- reach agreement with staff on the team leader's and individuals' roles in the development process
- provide on-going advice and feedback
- sometimes trade off immediate standards of performance for long-term development.

As you reflect upon the six styles, is there one you tend to predominantly use? Which do you rarely use? Do you make a conscious effort to think about the right approach for any given situation or do you rely on gut instinct? On the Leadership Matters website we have written a diagnostic tool called LM Styles which can help you and any of your colleagues better understand your preferred leadership styles and those which maybe are less well developed and could be great areas for personal growth.

Leaders at all levels need to be able to use a range of styles to suit their context and any particular situation. Sections A and B of this book stressed the importance of knowing yourself and understanding your situation, and some of your colleagues may require very different handling from others. It's always worth taking time to think about ways to bring out the best in the individuals in your teams. A competent but unconfident colleague may benefit from a coaching style of leadership. An able but resistant colleague may just need to be told what you expect from them, although in the long run this is probably neither acceptable nor sustainable.

Sometimes a team as a whole can need a very directional approach from a leader, particularly if it isn't functioning well. If you are working with a team of individuals that are not operating as a unit and where performance is variable, you may just need to say, 'we need to do it like this'. Getting the basics in place has to be the priority. If the situation in which you find yourself is in disarray, setting clear expectations around behaviour, teaching approaches, marking and homework are all areas where you may just need to be fairly directive to start with.

A high-performing team however, would find such an approach completely de-motivating. Coming in and telling people what to do would be a disaster. You need to reflect upon the capacity, competence and experience of your team. Knowing which style is best used with the team as a whole, or with different individuals within it, is where your professional judgement and emotional awareness as a leader come in. What is important is that you take the time to consciously think about which approach will build discretionary effort and have the overall impact you are seeking.

In Figure 64 I have attempted to summarise each of Goleman's six styles and when it might be appropriate to use each.

Style	Description	When useful	Correlation
Visionary	Communicating the goal; expectations on delivery	Pretty much anytime; set pieces and 1:1 dialogue	+0.54
Affiliative	Building and sustaining relationships	Again, always useful but especially if morale poor	+0.46
Directive	Telling people what to do, often in detail	Low capability or competence; no time	-0.26
Democratic	Sharing decision-making; delegating power	Confidence in the team; more time available	+0.43
Pacesetting	Copy me and keep up with me	When need fast change; show what's possible	-0.25
Coaching	Asking questions; focus on developing others	When you have time to build capacity in others	+0.42

Figure 64: Summary of different leadership styles and when to use them
Based on Goleman (2000)

Daniel Goleman's work also looked at the overall effectiveness of each of the six leadership styles. However, as the final column showing the correlation of each factor with a positive climate shows, it appears that two leadership styles can have a negative effect if they are overly-relied upon at the expense of the others. Goleman identified that the directive and pacesetting leadership styles had a negative impact on climate in the long term, even though there are times when this is absolutely the right approach to take. This is no surprise in a way. If, as a leader, you find yourself constantly leading by example or telling people what to do because you need to, you are working with people who maybe aren't suited to their roles and need to either improve fast or 'get off the bus'. On the other hand, if are using these styles but don't actually need to, you will be leading a team who feel you don't trust them and probably feel micro-managed.

As the data shows, Goleman also identified that the visionary and affiliative leadership styles were, on average, the most effective overall, closely followed by the democratic and coaching styles. However, a degree of caution has to be applied when using correlations like this, not least because the figures shown here are not always statistically significant.

Your school's journey

Taking a moment to think about your leadership approach and in particular the right style for your current context or situation, has the potential to make a big difference to the discretionary effort in your staff team. When it comes to thinking about the typical journey of improvement most schools (or teams) go through, I have come up with the simple model set out in Figure 65.

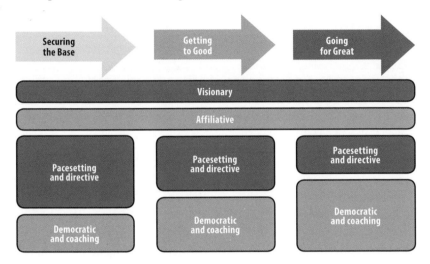

Figure 65: Changing leadership style over time

In all three stages, remembering that a visionary and affiliative leadership style is probably going to be useful in all contexts is a useful reminder in itself. But as this topic explored earlier, the degree to which you need to be pacesetting and directive ought to decline over time. Conversely, you should be gradually increasing how much you use the democratic and coaching leadership styles. To paraphrase Joel Klein, 'You can mandate adequacy, but you have to unleash greatness'.

The challenge for leaders at all levels is recognising when the context you are working in has improved, and then adapting your style to suit the change. Too often, leaders can get stuck with the leadership habits that served them well at the start of the journey and fail to make the necessary adjustments along the way.

Key points

- Have you developed a range of leadership styles that you use flexibly with different colleagues?
- Are there situations or individuals that would benefit from you using a different leadership style?
- Do you tend to just use one or two styles rather than the full range?
- Have you or colleagues changed your style over time to suit any change in context?

Topic 38

Ask first

The important thing is not to stop questioning. Curiosity has its own reason for existing.

Albert Einstein

In the end, leadership is about developing the right habits. As a school leader, I suspect you will be achieving your successes through a whole range of habits you don't even know you have. This topic looks at one leadership habit that I think underpins pretty much everything this book has been about: 'asking first'. If you want to understand yourself and your context better, you need to ask questions of yourself, others and your context. You need to interrogate or ask questions of the data you have at your disposal. Only by doing this are you in a position to identify what you need to make your priorities for action. And only then can you decide on how you will implement those actions to address the priorities: your leadership approach.

So how do you develop this important habit? Based on my experience of over 20 years in a range of senior leadership roles, I think school leaders at all levels only have three types of conversation! These are set out in Figure 66.

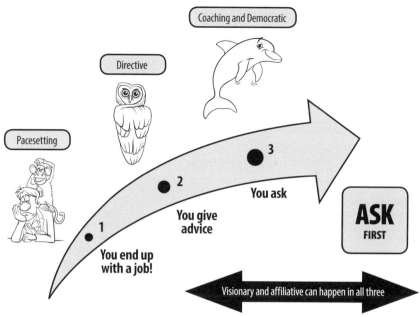

Figure 66: Ask First

'Monkey on the shoulder' conversations

In the first type, someone comes to talk to you about an issue or concern. Before you know it, you've ended up with a job! I call these your 'monkey on the shoulder' conversations where the monkey has quickly jumped from them onto you. Of course, there is a time and place where this is appropriate. If something is high-risk and looking like it is about to go wrong, you may well need to step in. If a colleague is really stressed for some reason and just can't cope, you need to help. But if your habit is to take on jobs from others without thinking, you aren't really leading, you are just doing.

I can remember as a young head of year, letting a huge number of monkeys jump on my back. Looking back there were a number of reasons why this tended to happen: firstly because I genuinely wanted to help out someone who I thought was very busy; secondly, because I wanted the other person to think I was capable and good at my job; thirdly, because it often felt, as I have mentioned before, that it would be quicker and easier to do something myself; and finally, because the reality of the culture in my school at the time was that heads of year were seen as firefighters, not team leaders. But as the thickness of the arrow on the model implies, while there is a place for type one conversations, you shouldn't have too many.

'Wise owl' conversations

The second type of conversation also has its place. These are dialogues in which you end up giving advice, making suggestions or even just telling someone what to do. At least with these, you don't end up with the job! Hopefully, the other person will be able to apply what they have learned from the conversation in the future. But if they keep coming back to you with similar questions, and if you continue to just answer them, they can become over-dependent upon you when it comes to making decisions. In this situation, these conversations don't build capacity or competence in your colleagues. In fact, they do the reverse.

'Dolphin' conversations

The third type of conversation, and the important habit I am suggesting all leaders need to keep developing, is that of *asking first*. In type three conversations, leaders just ask brilliant questions. Initially, these help you understand the situation; both the context and an individual's capacity to manage it. Only then can you decide the best way to proceed. If at this point you identify that you need to intervene and take the job off them or give them advice, then that's fine, you have made a conscious decision to do that. Not because it's what you are predisposed to do, but because it's what the situation needs. There is also the added benefit that the quality of your advice will be better because you know more about the situation.

Of course, if you both have time, spending a tiny bit longer on the conversation and staying in questioning mode can very often help people work out for themselves what they need to do. These mini-coaching conversations don't have to take long. It is more about you using a coaching leadership style than it is actually formal coaching.

Your will be surprised how, even in a one-minute conversation, how much of this ground can be covered. You leave the conversation with no task to undertake. Your colleague leaves feeling they have been properly listened to and having had the opportunity to think through the situation. They are also less likely to ask you the same question again next time.

If you are wondering why I have called these 'dolphin' conversations, I have to confess the rationale is somewhat tenuous. Basically, I wanted to keep the animal analogy going and dolphins do chat to one another a lot, so why wouldn't they ask each other questions? And anyway, they do use sonar to navigate, which is kind of like asking a question of the environment and seeing what comes back. Sorry, I said it was tenuous!

The link with Goleman's research

Daniel Goleman's 2001 work on leadership styles that we examined in Topic 37 is directly relevant here and lends some evidence in support of my *Ask First* model. If you think about it, in type one conversations you are pretty much adopting a pacesetting leadership style. Type two conversations broadly relate to you being directive. Both of these, on average and over time, were shown to have a negative effect on organisational climate where leaders overly relied upon them. However, type three conversations are much more akin to the democratic and coaching leadership styles, both of which, the evidence suggests, have a positive effect over time.

Naturally there are times when directive or pacesetting leadership is required, often in times of crisis when colleagues will look to you as a leader for guidance and direction. However, over time, the most effective leaders shift from leading in front of the team to leading the team from within.

As with *feedback tennis* which we examined in Topic 30 and *minding your Ps and Qs* from Topic 27, this is another very simple model but one that has the potential to really change leadership habits for the better. As with *feedback tennis*, this idea is still very much in its infancy as a concept, albeit built on some proven concepts from the field of positive psychology, so do get in touch if it's worked for you or offer me more appropriate feedback if it hasn't!

Key points

- Are you aware of the balance of type one, two and three conversations you have?
- Do you already have the habit of asking first or is this something you want to focus on?

Topic 39

Coaching approach

Listening is a positive act. You have
to put yourself out to do it.
David Hockney

In Topic 38 we looked at the three types of conversations that I suggest leaders have. Another way to look at these is through the lens of what Myles Downey (2004) calls the coaching continuum. I have adapted this to create Figure 67, which shows where I think type two (mentoring) and type three (coaching) fit within his model.

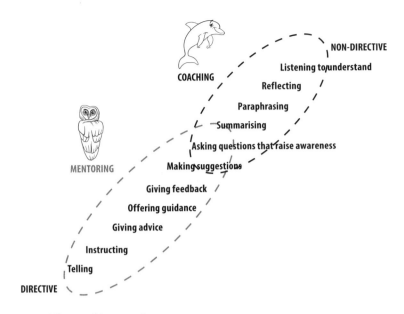

Figure 67: The coaching continuum
Adapted from Myles Downey (2004)

In keeping with the *Ask First* approach, one should aspire to keep to the top-right of the model and only move along the continuum when you judge it necessary. With inexperienced colleagues, taking the time to teach or show them how to do something is great, but it isn't a habit you want to adopt all the time or you run the risk of forgetting to lead!

Productive conversations

Having productive conversations with colleagues isn't just about having the right type of conversation. There is also something important about the way these conversations are conducted. To put it bluntly, what's it like talking to you? Figure 68 lists some key features that can really help conversations be more effective.

- ✓ Build rapport and empathy
- ✓ Show humility
- ✓ Listen and playback
- ✓ Be curious not judging
- ✓ Ask before you tell or model
- ✓ Be challenging but supportive
- ✓ Be positive and empowering

Figure 68: Features of productive conversations

Curious not judging

To pick up on one area from this table, ensuring you are curious not judging can make a real difference to what it's like to *talk to you*. You will know how it feels when someone you are talking to appears to be judging either you or what you are saying. We typically go into a more defensive mode and seek to protect our position. I am not saying that sometimes this isn't appropriate, but if this is your habit, you probably aren't going to help colleagues learn and grow as well as you might. Of course, there are times when a completely different type of very judgemental conversation is required, and Topic 32 focuses on how to have these often difficult conversations.

The importance of listening and playing back

As David Hockney reminds us, 'Listening is a positive act. You have to put yourself out to do it'. Even when you have developed the habit of asking great questions, if you don't listen actively, you will be missing the opportunity to be even more effective. It is not about being soft. Listening to colleagues can give you important information about what is really happening on the ground, it provides room for your team to grow and develop their thinking and is more likely to lead to distributed and sustainable leadership.

The first thing about listening is that it is active not passive. When done well, listening gives you more information about a situation or individual, and leads you towards greater insight, awareness and learning. You might see a different perspective or clarify your thinking. Active listening relies on good questioning. By structuring your questions, you can lead someone through a thinking process or suggest new ways of approaching a problem. How well do you tend to structure your questions at the moment? Are they leading or open? Do they provide enough space for the other person to reflect? Do your questions build on one another to lead to deeper learning?

You can also listen and pick up information that goes beyond the words being used. You can listen for emotion, body language, tone of voice, speed of talking and clarity of thinking. By listening actively for these, you can discern a great deal about the other person's frame of mind, emotional state and the purpose of the conversation. Often the words someone is using do not reflect what they really mean or want to say. How far do you listen beyond the words for what is really behind a conversation, what isn't being said?

How to show you are listening

Others are more likely to share if they feel that you are listening to them or that listening is resulting in some action or change. To a certain extent the relevance of your questions will demonstrate that you are listening. Techniques you can use to show listening include reflecting back the words someone has used or making statements showing you understand their emotions. Your body language and tone of voice can also mirror the non-verbal signals that they are giving. If they are angry you might choose to change your body language and tone of voice to make them non-confrontational; if they are upset you might again change them to elicit a different response.

Four levels of listening

The importance of actively listening is summarised well in Julie Starr's *four levels of listening* model in Figure 69. The further down the model you go the better your listening is and the more productive the outcomes.

Level	Activity of listener	What other person thinks
1. Attending	Eye contact and body language show interest	This person wants to listen to me
2. Accurate listening	Above – plus accurate paraphrasing of what other says	This person hears and understands what I am talking about
3. Empathetic listening	All of above – plus matching non-verbal cues with metaphor use & own feelings	This person knows what it feels like to be in my situation
4. Generative empathetic listening	All of above – plus the ability to use intuition & feelings to connect more fully & deeply with other person's situation	This person helps me to hear myself more fully than I can by myself – without telling me what to do, is helping me to find my own way.

Figure 69: Levels of listening
Adapted from *The coaching manual*, Julie Starr (2002)

To summarise the key content in this topic one need look no further than the excellent definition of coaching from Christian van Nieuwerburgh in his great book *The Leader's Guide to Coaching in Schools (2017)* which contains all the elements we have been discussing so far, as shown in Figure 70.

Coaching definition

A one-to-one conversation that focuses on the enhancement of **learning** and **development** through increasing **self-awareness** and a sense of personal **responsibility**, where the coach facilitates the **self-directed** learning of the coachee, through **questioning**, active **listening** and appropriate **challenge** in a **supportive** and encouraging environment.

Figure 70: A definition of coaching
Campbell and van Nieuwerburgh (2017)

Key points

- How good are you at using the range of techniques outlined in the coaching spectrum?
- Do you tend to be curious not judging?
- How good a listener are you? How do others know?

Topic 40

GROWTH coaching

Corridors, parking areas, playgrounds, staff rooms – these are all places where you and your staff have conversations every day. What if you could use these opportunities to build your staff resiliency and empower them to achieve their goals?

Growth Coaching International

Structuring your coaching conversations

For some *Ask First* conversations it may be useful to have a simple structure to help you organise the flow of the discussion. There are lots of models out there, none more well-known than John Whitmore's excellent 2009 GROW model. But more recently, a coaching model created specifically with schools in mind has emerged from Australia which works brilliantly for formal coaching sessions as well as everyday leadership dialogue. The GROWTH coaching model developed by Growth Coaching International (2016), has eight key stages, as shown in Figure 71.

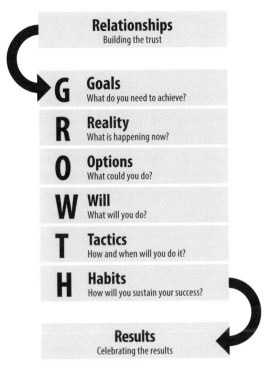

Figure 71: The GROWTH Coaching Model
Growth Coaching International (2016)

The first step in the model is to take time to build your **Relationship**. By ensuring good rapport and trust, you are likely to have a much more open and productive conversation.

You are then ready to help colleagues focus on the **Goal** they want to achieve. Getting them to frame this as precisely as possible can really help. I suspect creating clarity isn't a theme I need to dwell on if you have read to this point in the book! It can also be helpful to ask what the benefit of achieving the aim will be. If colleagues are clear about the benefits of a change, this really helps to increase the chances of it actually happening. So too can framing an aim in the future perfect tense – the sense that by a certain date they *will have* achieved their aim, rather than it being something they *will* do.

The second step is to review the **Reality** of the situation, so both you and your colleague have the chance to reflect on the current context. This can also have the benefit of allowing someone to 'let off steam' if this is needed! It also allows the person to start to organise their thoughts as well as enable you to ask questions based on what you are hearing that can get to the heart of an issue as well as continue to build rapport. Asking questions that direct the coachee to consider what's working and look to explore strengths and existing resources can also be particularly helpful at this stage and often leads to potential solutions.

Once the goal and context are clear, you can focus on their **Options** or their strategy. This part of the conversation is about exploring the possible ways of achieving their goal. It's worth really taking time on this. Just when you think they may have exhausted their ideas, a very powerful question can just be 'what else?' It's amazing what such a simple enquiry can elicit from colleagues. I often find it is at this point in a conversation that a really helpful new idea or strategy can emerge.

The next stage is to turn the options into the actions that colleagues are going to implement and, in particular, their very next steps. This is what they **Will** do. Linked to this are the **Tactics**. Pinning these down to specific dates and even times can help them avoid procrastination. Depending on the context, this part of the conversation can involve sketching out a rough plan of action. Very often however, just getting someone started on a next step can be all that's needed.

After this you need to help colleagues consider how whatever is going to happen or change is going to become a **Habit**. Asking about how they will sustain whatever they have decided to do can really make them focus on developing the right routines as an individual that will ensure ongoing benefit from the change.

The final step is to reflect on what has been useful and celebrate the **Results** of the conversation. While positive affirmations and encouragement can be incorporated at various points throughout the process, making sure you finish with this will hopefully help to leave your colleague feeling positive and upbeat about the future, as well as increase the probability that they will follow through on the actions they have committed to.

The final two topics have focused on two key, interrelated leadership habits: asking first and using a coaching leadership style. If the success of great school leadership depends on understanding context and situation and using this knowledge to determine what you need to do and how you need to do it, I hope you can see why I have chosen to end with these key skills. I know from my own experience as a school leader and from the hundreds of leaders I have worked with, that spending time on consciously improving your proficiency in these areas will pay dividends.

Key points

- Do you use a coaching model to help you structure your coaching conversations?
- Might the GROWTH coaching model be useful in your context?

Final thoughts

Excellence is an art won by training and
habituation. We do not act rightly because
we have virtue or excellence, but we
rather have those because we have acted
rightly. We are what we repeatedly do.
Excellence, then, is not an act but a habit.
Aristotle

In writing this third edition, I have become increasingly convinced that it
is actually the development of the right leadership habits that makes the
biggest difference to the effectiveness of school leaders and their impact
on pupil outcomes. Every day I visit schools where I have the privilege to
reflect on what these leaders are up to on a routine basis.

This final part of the book is my attempt to summarise what I think are,
if you asked me to choose from everything in this book, the top six habits
that leaders might prioritise. While being influenced by research and
evidence, this is more of a personal view of what seems to me to represent
the habits demonstrated by the most successful leaders at all levels within
our school system.

Figure 72: Six habits for success

Great leaders create clarity

Your staff team will be more motivated if they know what is expected of them and you give them the chance to get good at stuff. There is nothing worse for staff than not being clear about 'the way we do things around here' or if things are always changing. Are you clear about those things that you expect to be done uniformly and those where there is scope to work more flexibly within a set of guiding principles? Do you take every opportunity to reinforce clarity and check for understanding? It's the first step in creating consistent outcomes for pupils.

More on this in Topic 17 (Clarity).

Great leaders expect quality

Selling and modelling an inspiring vision for the future is a powerful motivator for staff. If you have the habit of taking every opportunity to reinforce this vision through your everyday conversations, you will know the powerful effect this can have, especially if you are always on the lookout to celebrate and highlight when colleagues are demonstrating what these expectations look like. How well do you reinforce the highest expectations of yourself and everyone else in every conversation you have?

More on this in Topic 22 (Little things matter).

Great leaders plan ahead

Stepping off the dance-floor and taking a look from the balcony is a vital habit for any leader. Seeing this bigger picture enables leaders to take a longer-term view to planning and strategy. It also means you can create a strong, more stable culture because implementation is properly thought through and not rushed. There is nothing staff hate more – and therefore buy into less – than a last-minute and rushed new idea. Finally, good planning forces good prioritisation, which with workloads as they are, has to be a good thing.

More on this in Topics 33 (Prioritisation), 34 (Managing change), 35 (Checklists) and 36 (Personal organisation).

Great leaders enable others

Leading is all about bringing out the best in others, helping them to lead with you on your journey together. This involves building trust, capacity and confidence in others. It also involves developing the habit of *letting go*. Some leaders find this habit harder to develop than others! The knowledge that you can quite often do something faster and better than a busy colleague is often a barrier to giving them opportunities. How good are you at empowering your staff, not only at delegating projects but also the decisions involved when actually working on them?

More on this in Topics 25 (Teams and teamwork) and 26 (Delegation).

Great leaders keep it positive

Whatever your own thoughts and emotions are, keeping a focus on the positive – however hard this may sometimes be – can make a real difference to how staff are feeling. Great leaders have the habit of focusing on how far you have come and the positive future you are headed to, creating a more can-do culture and a more optimistic climate. Focusing on the problems you currently face does exactly the opposite. That's not to say these leaders ignore the challenges, it just means they acknowledge them and then focus on what's to be done and the benefit of doing it.

More on this in Topics 7 (Courage and resilience), 22 (Little things matter) and 39 (Coaching approach).

Great leaders *ask* first

The one leadership habit that I think underpins pretty much everything great leaders do is 'asking first'. If you want to understand yourself and your context better, you need to ask questions of yourself, others and your context. You need to interrogate or ask questions of the data you have at your disposal. Only by doing this are you in a position to identify what you need to make your priorities for action. And only then can you decide on how you will implement these priorities: your leadership approach. The everyday habit is about asking questions at the start of most conversations, rather than straightaway giving advice or taking on a job yourself. This also has the advantage of making staff feel listened to, valued and cared for.

More on this in Topic 38 (Ask first).

And finally...

School leadership is a remarkable privilege. There are very few leadership roles where what you do, at whatever level, makes such a real difference to other people's lives. With all its ups and downs, leading in schools can be a terrifically rewarding job. Even now, many years after headship, I still get to hear back from former pupils about what they are up to. Just the fact they want me to know is the best reminder, if one were needed, that what we do as teachers, support staff and leaders makes more difference than we will ever know.

On one level, in writing this third edition of *Leadership Matters*, I hope I have provided you with a comprehensive set of practical tools you can use in school, underpinned by a useful set of theoretical frameworks and models. Throughout, my aim has been to take the complex and make it simple without making it simplistic. I think someone called Einstein may have come up with that elegant concept!

But more than that, I hope I have inspired you in the next stage in your own personal leadership journey, wherever that may take you and the pupils you serve.

As Steve Radcliffe would say: 'Be up to something!'

Key references

Ancona, D., Malone, T.W., Orlikowski, W.J., and Senge, P.M. (2007) 'In praise of the incomplete leader'. *Harvard Business Review* February 2007 (2) pp 109-118. Available at: https://hbr.org/2007/02/in-praise-of-the-incomplete-leader (Accessed 15 Jun. 2018).

Bambrick-Santoyo, P. (2012) *Leverage Leadership: a practical guide to building exceptional schools.* San Francisco: Jossey-Bass.

Black, P. and Wiliam, D. (1998) Inside the Black Box: Raising Standards Through Classroom Assessment. *Phi Delta Kappan* 80 (2) pp 139–144, 146–148.

Brighouse, T. (2007) *How successful head teachers survive and thrive.* Abingdon: RM Publications.

Brighouse, T. and Woods, D. (2008) *What makes a good school now?* London: Network Continuum.

Campbell, A. (2015) *Winners: And how they succeed.* London: Hutchinson.

Campbell, J. and van Nieuwerburgh, C. (2017) *The Leader's Guide to Coaching in Schools.* Thousand Oaks, CA: Corwin.

Clough, P. and Strycharczyk, D. (2012) *Developing Mental Toughness: Improving Performance, Wellbeing and Positive Behaviour in Others.* London: Kogan Page.

Coffield, F., Moseley, D., Hall, E., and Ecclestone, K. (2004) *Learning styles and pedagogy in post-16 learning. A systematic and critical review.* London: Learning and Skills Research Centre.

Collins, J. (2001) *Good to great.* New York: Collins Business.

Corporate Leadership Council (2004) *Driving Performance and Retention Through Employee Engagement.* Available at: http://cwfl.usc.edu/assets/pdf/Employee%20 engagement.pdf (Accessed 15 Jun. 2018).

Covey, S. (2004) *7 habits of highly effective people.* London: Simon and Schuster.

Covey, S. (2008) *The speed of trust. One thing that changes everything.* London: Simon and Schuster.

Department for Education (2016a) *Expert group report on continuing professional development.* London: The Stationery Office.

Department for Education (2016b) *Standard for teachers' professional development.* London: The Stationery Office.

Downey, M. (2003) *Effective Coaching: Lessons from the Coach's Coach.* London: Texere Publishing.

Drucker, P. (2007) *Essential Drucker: management, the individual and society.* New York: Routledge.

Dudley, P. (2014) *Lesson study: professional learning for our time.* New York: Routledge.

Dweck, C. (2012) *Mindset: How You Can Fulfil Your Potential.* New York: Ballantine Books.

Education Endowment Foundation (2014) *Teaching and Learning Toolkit.* Available at: https://educationendowmentfoundation.org.uk/evidence-summaries/teaching-learning-toolkit (Accessed 15 Jun. 2018).

Education Endowment Foundation (2015) *Making the best use of teaching assistants.* Available at: https://educationendowmentfoundation.org.uk/tools/making-best-use-of-teaching-assistants/guidance-report/ (Accessed 15 Jun. 2018).

Fullan, M. (2001) *Leading the culture of change.* San Francisco: Jossey-Bass.

Fullan, M. (2008) *The six secrets of change.* San Francisco: Jossey-Bass.

Gawande, A. (2011) *The Checklist Manifesto: How to Get Things Right.* New York: Henry Holt.

Goleman, D. (1995) *Emotional Intelligence: Why it Can Matter More Than IQ.* London: Bloomsbury.

Goleman, D. (2000) *Leadership that gets results. Harvard Business Review* March-April 2000 (03) pp 78-90. Available at: https://hbr.org/2000/03/leadership-that-gets-results (Accessed 15 Jun. 2018).

Goleman, D., Boyatzis, R.E., and McKee, A. (2002) *The new leaders.* London: Little, Brown.

Growth Coaching International (2016) Available at: http://www.growthcoaching.com.au/the-growth-approach.html (Accessed 15 Jun. 2018).

Handy, C. (1997) *The hungry spirit.* London: Hutchinson.

Hargreaves, D. (2011) *Leading a self-improving school system: towards maturity.* NCSL. Available at: https://www.gov.uk/government/publications/a-self-improving-school-system-towards-maturity (Accessed 15 Jun. 2018).

Hattie, J. (2009) *Visible Learning: A Synthesis of Over 800 Meta-Analyses Relating to Achievement.* New York: Routledge.

Hay Group (2007) *Rush to the top: Accelerating the development of leaders in schools.* Available at: https://www.haygroup.com/downloads/uk/Rush_to_the_Top_low_res.pdf (Accessed 15 Jun. 2018).

Heifetz, R. and Linsky, M. (2002) *Leadership on the Line: Staying Alive through the Dangers of Leading.* Boston: Harvard Business School Press.

House of Commons Education Committee (2017) *Multi-academy trusts.* Education Select Committee Report. Available at: https://publications.parliament.uk/pa/cm201617/cmselect/cmeduc/204/204.pdf (Accessed 15 Jun. 2018).

Jones, G. (2016) *Evidence Based Management, The Basic Principles.* Amsterdam: The Centre for Evidence Based Management.

Kahneman, D. (2012) *Thinking, fast and slow.* London: Penguin.

Katzenbach, J.R. and Smith, D.K. (2003) *The Wisdom of Teams: Creating the High-Performance Organization.* Boston: Harvard Business School Press.

Kilmann, R. (1994) *Producing useful knowledge for organisations.* San Francisco: Jossey-Bass.

Knoster, T., Villa R. and Thousand, J. (2000) *A framework for thinking about systems change.* Baltimore: Paul H. Brookes Publishing Co.

Koch, R. (1998) *The 80/20 Principle: The Secret of Achieving More with Less.* New York: Doubleday.

Kotter, J. P. (1996) *Leading change.* Boston: Harvard Business Review Press.

Kübler-Ross, E. (1969) *On death and dying.* New York: Scribner.

Leithwood, K., Day, C., Sammons, P., Harris, A. and Hopkins, D. (2006) *Seven strong claims about successful school leadership.* Nottingham: National College for School Leadership.

Lencioni, P. M. (2002) *The five dysfunctions of a team; a leadership fable.* San Francisco: Jossey-Bass.

Lencioni, P. M. (2012) *The Advantage.* San Francisco: Jossey-Bass.

Luft, J. and Ingham, H. (1955) *The Johari window, a graphic model of interpersonal awareness.* Los Angeles: University of California.

McGregor, D. (1960) *The Human Side of Enterprise.* New York: McGraw-Hill.

Matthews, P. (2009) *Twelve outstanding secondary schools.* Ofsted. Available at: http://dera.ioe.ac.uk/11232/ (Accessed 15 Jun. 2018).

Matthews, P. (2017) *The power of incremental coaching – improving teacher quality. Professional Development Today* 19 (1).

Mehrabian, A. (1972) *Nonverbal Communication.* New Brunswick: Aldine Transaction.

Muijs, D. and Reynolds, D. (2011) *Effective Teaching: Evidence and Practice.* London: Sage.

National Governors' Association (2015) *A Framework for Governance.* Available at: https://www.nga.org.uk/Services/Clerking-Matters/Clerk-to-governors/Framework-for-Governance.aspx (Accessed 15 Jun. 2018).

NCSL (2003) *Heart of the matter: a practical guide to what middle leaders can do to improve learning in secondary schools.* Available at: bit.ly/2KtMvrD (Accessed 15 Jun. 2018).

NCSL (2004) *A model of school leadership in challenging urban environments.* Available at: http://dera.ioe.ac.uk/5276/7/download_id%3D17300%26filename%3Dmodel-of-school-leadership-in-challenging-urban-environments_Redacted.pdf (Accessed 15 Jun. 2018).

Pendleton, D. and Furnham, A. (2012) *Leadership: all you need to know.* Basingstoke: Palgrave Macmillan.

Pink, D.H. (2011) *Drive: the surprising truth about what motivates us.* New York: Riverhead Books.

Radcliffe, S. (2012) *Leadership: plain and simple.* (2nd ed.) Edinburgh: Pearson.

Reynolds, D. (2004) *Within-school variation: its extent and causes.* Available at: http://www.highreliabilityschools.co.uk/_resources/files/downloads/within-school-variation/dr2004a1.pdf (Accessed 15 Jun. 2018).

Robertson Cooper (2018) *The i-resilience report.* Available at: https://www.robertsoncooper.com/ (Accessed 15 Jun. 2018).

Robinson, V. (2011) *Pupil centred leadership.* San Francisco: Jossey-Bass.

Scott, S. (2003) *Fierce conversations.* London: Piatkus.

Sherrington, T. (2017) *Blogs on workload.* Available at: https://teacherhead.com/tag/workload/ (Accessed 15 Jun. 2018).

Sinek, S. (2011) *Start with why. How great leaders inspire everyone to take action.* New York: Penguin.

Starr, J. (2002) *The coaching manual.* London: Pearson.

Strong, M., Gargani, J. and Hacifazlioğluet, O. (2011) Do we know a successful teacher when we see one? Experiments in the identification of successful teachers. *Journal of Teacher Education* 62 (4) pp. 367–382. Available at http://journals.sagepub.com/doi/abs/10.1177/0022487110390221 (Accessed 15 Jun. 2018).

Tuckman, B. (1965) Developmental sequence in small groups. *Psychological Bulletin* 63 (6) pp. 384–99.

Ward, S. (2009) *Time management types.* Available at: http://sbinfocanada.about.com/cs/timemanagement/a/timetypes.htm (Accessed 15 Jun. 2018).

Watkins, M. (2003) *The first 90 days.* Boston: Harvard Business Review Press.

Whitmore, J. (2009) *Coaching for performance GROWing Human Potential and Purpose – the Principles and Practice of Coaching and Leadership.* (4th ed.) London: Nicholas Brealy.

Wiliam, D. (2015) The research delusion. *Times Educational Supplement* 10 April 2015.

Yerkes, R.M. and Dodson, J.D. (1908) The relation of strength of stimulus to rapidity of habit-formation. *Journal of Comparative Neurology and Psychology* 18 (5) pp. 459–482. Available at: http://www.viriya.net/jabref/the_relation_of_strength_of_stimulus_to_rapidity_of_habit-formation.pdf (Accessed 15 Jun. 2018).